Best wishes
Christmas '93

Pleasant memories!
that will test you
sense of humour!

Dave & the J J's

Ian Cover was born in 1956 and grew up in Geelong, Victoria, where as an off-spinner with Highton Methodists he topped the club averages in 1970-71, capturing 17 wickets at 14.470588.

Two summers ago, Ian came out of retirement for a social match against the English press and snared the prize wicket of the BBC's Christopher Martin-Jenkins. Ian has since resisted offers to take up a coaching position with an unnamed English county side.

Ian is also a journalist, broadcaster and professional sports spectator. He is perhaps most notably a member of the highly acclaimed radio troupe, the Coodabeen Champions. He is married with one child.

Mervyn Hughes was born in 1961 and grew up in country Victoria and the outer Melbourne suburb of Werribee. He has been a regular member of the Australian Test squad since 1988, and has now joined the select few Australian bowlers to take over 200 Test wickets.

He is married and lives in Melbourne.

By Merv Hughes & Ian Cover

IRONBARK

First published in Ironbark hardback by Pan Macmillan Publishers
Australia 1993
a division of Pan Macmillan Australia Pty Limited
63-71 Balfour Street, Chippendale, Sydney

National Library of Australia
Cataloguing-in-Publication data:

Cover, Ian.
Merv and me.
ISBN 0330 274 643
1. Cricket - Humor. I. Hughes, Merv. II. Title
796.3580207

Typeset in 12/15pt Andover by Midland Typesetters, Australia
Printed in Australia by McPherson's Print Group

Contents

Acknowledgements

Three years ago, I dedicated my first book to the many close friends I had made through sport. This time, I'd like to acknowledge the people who have assisted my cricket career through their generous sponsorship. As it turns out, they're more than sponsors, they're good friends, too. Thanks go to: Broadmeadows Leisure Centre (Sam and the crew), Competitive Edge Sports Management (David Emerson), Coopers and Lybrand (Geoff Collinson), Easton Sports (Swan Richards), FOX-FM (the Morning Crew), Musashi (Jamie Mitchell), Oakley (Sandy Kempsey), Puma (John Forbes), Tubemakers Australia (Hugh Macdonald) and Werribee Mazda (Chris, Joe and the team). — MH

From my part, I'd like to thank James Fraser at Pan Macmillan Publishers Australia for the opportunity; Michael Langley for editing duties; and David Emerson for advice and encouragement. Thanks also to Steve Marshall, Andrew Goddard and Mike Walsh for their contributions. And Merv, for keeping the diary and getting me the tickets. — IC

Forewords

I

BIG Merv? He a funny boy. The first time he come to my restaurant, I say to my wife Constanza, 'Now there's a boy who likes his pasta.' He was there with the other Aussie cricketers, and when I go to their table and ask for the order, Big Merv say, 'I'll have the Spaghetti Bolognese, the Canneloni Napoletana, the Tagliatelle e Spinacci, the Pasticcio de Marcheroni con Salsa Verde and the homemade Lasagna. But just the entree size – I gotta watch my weight.'

He a funny boy. I hear he from Melbourne, and I say to him, 'Hey, Big Merv! My cousin Santino live in Melbourne. You must know him, eh?' Big Merv, he just say, 'Hey Wally! All I know is that there ain't too many scallops in Boonie's scallopine . . . '

My sister Bella, we call her 'PMM' – Pasta-Making Machine – because she make all our pasta by hand – she loves Big Merv. But since Big Merv been eating at my restaurant, Bella been on Workcare with bad case of RSI. Ah, he a funny boy.

The only time I ever have any trouble with Big Merv was the night he enjoy his meal so much, he go up to the chef

– my other cousin Luciano – and stick the tongue in his ear. After I manage to get the meat cleaver out of Luciano's hand, I have to tell Big Merv that the last man who try that with Luciano, he sleep with the fishes now – understand?

Big Merv, he a funny boy. But we proud to make him honorary member of the Gambino Family.

Volare ('Wally') Gambino
Proprietor
Gambino's Trattoria
London, England

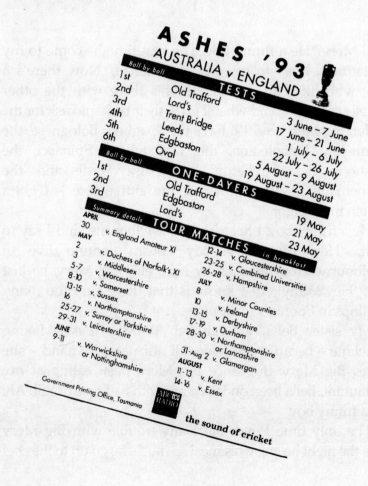

ASHES '93
AUSTRALIA v ENGLAND

TESTS

Ball-by-ball		
1st	Old Trafford	3 June – 7 June
2nd	Lord's	17 June – 21 June
3rd	Trent Bridge	1 July – 6 July
4th	Leeds	22 July – 26 July
5th	Edgbaston	5 August – 9 August
6th	Oval	19 August – 23 August

ONE-DAYERS

Ball by ball		
1st	Old Trafford	19 May
2nd	Edgbaston	21 May
3rd	Lord's	23 May

TOUR MATCHES
Summary details — *in breakfast*

APRIL				
30	v. England Amateur XI	12-14	v. Gloucestershire
MAY		23-25	v. Combined Universities
2	v. Duchess of Norfolk's XI	26-28	v. Hampshire
3	v. Middlesex	JULY	
5-7	v. Worcestershire	8	v. Minor Counties
8-10	v. Somerset	10	v. Ireland
13-15	v. Sussex	13-15	v. Derbyshire
16	v. Northamptonshire	17-19	v. Durham
25-27	v. Surrey or Yorkshire	28-30	v. Northamptonshire or Lancashire
29-31	v. Leicestershire	31-Aug 2	v. Glamorgan
JUNE		AUGUST	
9-11	v. Warwickshire or Nottinghamshire	11-13	v. Kent
		14-16	v. Essex

Government Printing Office, Tasmania

ABC RADIO

the sound of cricket

II

*'Never in the history of human endeavour has so much been
ordered and consumed by so few.'*
– Nigel Q. Farquhar, Manager, Guest Relations and
Room Service, Nottingham Tropicana Hotel,
23 August 1975

SOME men are born Room Service Waiters. Others choose to
be Room Service Waiters. And some men have Room
Service Waiting thrust upon them. Room service is not a
career for the faint of heart or the thin of skin. As proved
during the 1975 Ashes tour of England by Ian Chappell's
Australians. That tour was the testing ground where
many fine young men and women, most straight out of
Mini-Bar Replenishment or Bed Linen, went on to prove
their mettle in the trench warfare that is Room Service at the
highest level.

I must confess there were times in '75 when the mere
thought of 'Seven burgers, two dozen cans and another
carton of Craven A to the Walters/Gilmour Room' made
even hardened cases like myself pine for the relative
security of the Concierge Desk.

Ah yes, those were the days. When men were men and
English fast bowlers weren't raised in Perth. Not like
today's new breed of Aussie cricketers! Fine young
gentlemen, one and all. Especially that Mervyn Hughes.
Terrific lad! Quiet, humble, courteous. Many's the time
he'd dial Room Service and, after apologising for the
lateness of the hour, politely request 'a bucket of ice for
my knee and a couple of ripe lemons for Warnie's hair'. I tell
you, with guests like Merv Hughes, it's a pleasure to say,
'Coming right up, sir.'

Barrington Smythe Thomas-Thompson
President, British Room Service Waiters Guild

III

IT is well-known fact that all Test cricketers regardless of race, creed, colour or religion, love to eat Indian food. Especially those Australian boys. They know how to give and take a bit of the good hot curry. And when they're in England, where do they go for a good vindaloo? They come to see me, the world famous Nawab of Orkney.

Let me introduce myself. I am Ramesh Krishnan Ben Patel Kingsley, known to my many friends in the international cricket community as 'Woofer'. Together with my wife June, I own the world famous Pungent Pappadam of the Punjab Indian Restaurant. Over the years, I have rubbed shoulders with some of the finest cricketers in the world. And a few English batsmen as well (heh heh).

Last time the Aussie boys come to my restaurant, that big fast bowler Merv Hughes walks in wearing the British Raj khaki short pants and a zebra-pattern short-sleeved shirt. Absolute shocker! Anyway, at about course 13 in my world famous 19-course Punjab banquet (please order before noon) he picks up one of my world famous giant pappadams and says, 'Hey Woofer, what's this? Looks like a frisbee and tastes like a Samboy chip.'

'You great alec,' I say. 'Take a good hard look at yourself. You look like Daktari and bowl like Kamahl.' Heh heh. Even Simmo smiled at that one. Ever since then, me and Merv been good mates. It's an honour for him to have met me.

Ramesh Krishnan Ben Patel Kingsley
Proprietor
Pungent Pappadam of the Punjab
Orkney West
England

Introduction

MERV Hughes and I go back a long way. More than 25 years, in fact. Well, sort of. Let me explain . . .

Back in the early 1960s, my oldest brother, Harold, graduated from teachers college and, for his first posting, was appointed to the staff of the Apollo Bay Consolidated School. A couple of the teachers were members of the local cricket team and they invited Harold to join the club. He didn't play the game but thought by getting involved as the club's secretary it would be a great way to meet the people of the Victorian coastal township.

As a youngster, I was impressed that my brother had such an important position with a cricket club. I was even more impressed when one day he invited me to accompany him to watch the team play. As I recall, Apollo Bay were visiting Birregurra, a dairying hamlet in the heart of Cliff Young territory not too far away. I also recall that the boys from the Bay looked resplendent in their red caps and I felt rather good to be wearing one as I roamed the boundary line watching the action.

Alas, I can't recall much of that action apart from the sight of a burly, dark-haired fast bowler roaring in from the end where my brother had parked the car. My brother said, 'This is the big bloke I was telling you about. Watch him, he'll sort 'em out.' The bowler's name was Hughes. Ian Hughes.

1

A couple of decades later, I wandered into St Kilda's Junction Oval in Melbourne where Victoria was playing a Sheffield Shield match. There had been much talk about Merv and his position in the state team, and newspaper stories were using phrases such as 'moment of truth', 'under the hammer' and 'acid test' in close promixity to the name Hughes.

Funnily enough, I'd never seen Merv in action, in the flesh, as it were. On this particular day in late 1988, I didn't have to wait long, for the big fellow was operating from the Fitzroy Street end when I arrived. In fact, he was just turning at the top of his run-up. As he leaned forward and pushed off from his mark, I was suddenly transported back in time to that cricket ground in Birregurra . . . Ian Hughes, Merv Hughes, I wondered if they were related?

As cricket fans the world over have come to know, Merv Hughes produces the goods when the pressure is at its greatest and that was the situation he found himself in on this day. He duly responded at the Junction Oval, taking 7/81. The media reports quickly changed tack. 'Moment of truth' and all that was replaced with 'thrust his name in front of the national selectors'!

Some time later, I met Merv for the first time. Subsequently, our paths crossed in radio studios and at sports lunches and dinners. Many times, as I was driving home, I'd realise that I'd forgotten to ask Merv if he was related to Ian Hughes, the bloke I'd seen opening the bowling for Apollo Bay against Birregurra. Finally, as I was chatting to Merv for an article about his favourite football team, Footscray, I remembered the question.

'Yeah, Apollo Bay, we lived there once,' Merv said. 'I'll check with the old man.' He rang back, confirmed the sighting, and another piece of cricketing trivia went into my memory bank filed under the heading Stuff That Could Be Handy For A Merv Hughes Book One Day. Not that I ever imagined that I'd be involved in a Merv Hughes book. That was until someone heard that I was heading for England to watch some of the 1993 Ashes series.

My limited knowledge of the publishing business was that these projects are usually cooked up during a round of golf or over a long lunch. In this case, it was both. On 17 March, during a round of golf at Huntingdale, Melbourne, just weeks after the Australian Masters had been staged there, the idea was put to me; four weeks later I sat down to lunch with Merv and mapped out the book.

'I've even bought a diary,' Merv enthused.

'I hope you got a discount – we're a third of the way through the year,' I said.

'I know that. Do you think I'm thick or something?' Merv retorted, before giving me the sort of glare which is normally reserved for a batsman who has just snicked him through the vacant third slip.

'Listen,' he continued, 'I've got the diary and I've already started writing. I think the diary is the way to go. I'll get it copied before I leave. Not a problem.'

Merv sprinkles his conversations with the statement that this or that is 'not a problem' like he peppers batsmen with bouncers. And if he says something is 'not a problem', then I'm not going to argue with him. Besides, he's bigger than me, a lot bigger.

The only time I ever disagreed with him was at the launch of a new type of cricket ball when he suggested it would make a good photo opportunity if I was to face up to him in the nets. Now, for me, that was a problem!

So, the diary was agreed to, along with the idea that I

3

would provide some observations from the other side of the fence. The fan's perspective as a contrast and complement to Merv's inside view. Or to borrow from that colourful politician Don Chipp, I'd be keeping the bastard honest. Merv is a leg-puller from way back and he could write anything in the diary and get away with it.

As promised, Merv handed over the early pages of the diary on Saturday 24 April, just hours before boarding the plane to England with his 16 Australian teammates. Excitedly, I flicked through the pages and cast my eyes upon the first entry, reproduced here.

April 1993

1 Thursday   Week 13 • 091/274

7.00

8.00

      NOT MUCH

9.00

10.00

11.00

12.00

1.00

2.00

3.00

4.00

5.00

6.00

7.00

January 1993	February	March	April	May	June

4

'Thanks heaps,' I said, 'that's the sort of stuff we need to write a book. Just one thing – can you be a bit briefer.'

Due to the fact that this is a family book, I can't repeat Merv's reply, but suffice to say it contained as many words as his first diary entry. However, he promised that once he sat down on the plane he would have plenty of time to write and, he assured me, it would get better.

'Well, don't worry about last night. I'll do that,' I said helpfully. Last night had been the farewell dinner for the team, an evening arranged by the Australian Cricket Board and the tour sponsor. As luck would have it, the ACB invited me to perform the duties as master of ceremonies for the night.

Stepping out of the lift on the Regent Hotel's 35th floor, I don't know who was more excited, me or the players. Sure, I knew Merv and the other Victorians – Shane Warne and Paul Reiffel – but here I was rubbing shoulders with the cream of Australia's cricketers, sporting heroes I'd only ever seen from the other side of the fence or on TV. Above all, as a Coodabeen Champion, it was an enormous thrill to be in the company of a genuine champion, Allan Border.

Much of the talk over pre-dinner drinks was about the snappy business suits worn by the players. They would still wear the traditional Australian cricket blazers to meet the Queen, but the suits had been added to their wardrobes for occasions such as this dinner. Ian Healy and physiotherapist Errol Alcott were behind the move and they were being referred to as the team's fashion consultants. The verdict from the team was a big thumbs-up.

As well as canvassing opinions on the new suits, I took the opportunity to move around and meet as many of the players as possible for another important reason. Get to know them, I thought, and you're a chance for a spare ticket to Lord's. Spotting a player on his own, I sidled up to him and said, 'Congratulations, Damien.' The player in question gave me a funny look. Suddenly, I realised why – it was Michael Slater. My face reddened as a couple of tickets fluttered out the window.

After drinks, the fifty or so guests moved in to the Regent's West Tower Suite to dine at a table as long as a cricket pitch. Down one end of the room was a small table with a replica of the Ashes urn sitting in a glass case – just to remind the players what the next four months were all about.

There were a few more reminders during the evening as Australian Cricket Board chairman Alan Crompton wished the team well, ABC Radio commentator Neville Oliver reminisced about the 1989 triumph and a couple of videos of the Wallabies' rugby successes were shown. Coach Bobby Simpson had his say, too, congratulating the selectors and expressing his confidence that the Ashes would be retained.

I also threw in a few reminders of my own; reminders that I was preparing to make my debut as a spectator at Lord's and that a couple of tickets wouldn't go astray. From the lectern, I could see a half-whince, half-grimace come over Merv's face. 'You're going to come looking for me when the ticket crunch comes, aren't you?' he growled later. I umm-ed and ahh-ed, waiting to hear him say, 'Not a problem' but he said nothing.

The highlight of the night was a special presentation by the ACB to Allan Border to mark his becoming the highest run scorer in the history of Test cricket. He had passed Sunil Gavaskar's 10,122 during the first Test in New Zealand a few weeks earlier.

Border has never cared much for individual records or

personal milestones, but he obviously appreciated this gesture. The presentation included two cricket bats signed by 17 of the all-time top run-getters. At the top of the blade, there was room for Border to sign his own name. Seeing the chance for a unique claim to fame, I grabbed a pen from my suit pocket and thrust it towards the great man only to be beaten by a lunging Alan Crompton.

The bats were accompanied by a leather-bound book containing messages from the batsmen whose names were on the bats. Oh, and someone had snared, mounted and engraved the ball which Border hit for four in New Zealand to pass Gavaskar.

The salute to the skipper wound up with another video, this time featuring him in action from his debut in 1978 right up to the just-completed series against the West Indies and New Zealand. It was great stuff. I'd forgotten how many times during his early years that he'd belted bowlers through point with a quick yet powerful flick of the wrists or punched them through midwicket with that famous short-arm jab.

There was some rare footage of him standing up to a short-pitched assault from the West Indies pace attack on their home soil. Gee, I thought, he's been through a few battles, old AB, and another campaign is about to start. You could feel the admiration for him coming from around the table. I'm sure the young players, particularly those making their first tour of England, were inspired.

For a man who doesn't show much emotion publicly, AB appeared to get a little choked up for once. About halfway through the video, he got up and went to the toilet. When he came back, he sat on his own at one end of the room watching one of the television monitors. In a moment of private reflection, he was probably thinking, 'Yeah, I have been through a lot, haven't I?'

New ACB chief executive Graham Halbish's instructions were that the night should be a mixture of relaxation, fun and motivation. As far as I was concerned, you could forget the relaxation and fun after watching the Border tape. I, for one, was ready to put the pads on.

The next day, I stood on the viewing deck at Tullamarine airport and waved goodbye to flight QF9, the Qantas Jumbo carrying the Australian cricket team on its quest to retain the Ashes. In seven weeks' time, it would be my turn to board the same flight en route to fulfilling a lifelong ambition of watching Australia and England playing a Test match at Lord's. During those ensuing seven weeks, Merv set about writing the diary, recovering from the recent surgery on his right knee and, occasionally, playing cricket. Feeling like a teacher checking on a lazy student's homework, I phoned Merv frequently to ask how the writing was going. The answer, as always, was 'Not a problem'.

What follows is Merv's 1993 Ashes tour diary. As the title *Merv And Me* suggests, I've had my two bob's worth in the writing of the book and my comments are dropped in among Merv's diary entries and a selection of letters sent to Merv while on tour (yes, they are for real!). To aid your understanding of just who the big fellow is talking about, here is a list of the 17 players, the manager, coach and physiotherapist and the nicknames Merv uses when he refers to them.

Australian Touring Party by Nickname

AB	*Allan Border (captain)*
Babsie	*David Boon*
Billy	*Craig McDermott*
BJ	*Brendon Julian*

Cracka	*Wayne Holdsworth*
Ger	*Des Rundle (manager)*
Heals	*Ian Healy*
Hooter	*Errol Alcott (physiotherapist)*
Junior	*Mark Waugh*
Marto	*Damien Martyn*
Maysie	*Tim May*
Pistol	*Paul Reiffel*
Simmo	*Bob Simpson (coach)*
Slats	*Michael Slater*
Swervin'	*Merv Hughes*
Tubby	*Mark Taylor (vice-captain)*
Tugga	*Steve Waugh*
Unit	*Matthew Hayden*
Warnie	*Shane Warne*
Ziggy	*Tim Zoehrer*

1 Getting There and Getting Ready

Saturday 24 April: Melbourne

Flight leaves at 4.10 pm, so do the last-minute running around. Life's been like that for the past three weeks since getting back from New Zealand. Lots of running around.

Since the knee operation, I've been going to the gym as part of the rehabilitation process. Then there's been promotional work and lots of meetings. I've also been trying to catch up with all the domestic stuff that gets neglected over summer while travelling around playing cricket for Victoria and Australia. Things like mowing the lawn, washing the car, knocking down a fence and tidying up around the place.

And, most importantly, I've been spending some time with my wife Sue. In turn, we've been catching up with family and friends. Been to a few barbecues as well as hosting a couple ourselves. Come to think of it, the last three weeks have been a bit of a blur. Must suggest to Cove that we call the first chapter The Three-Week Blur.

The phone rings a few times during the final packing. One of the callers is Dean Jones, who wishes me all the best for the tour. Deano was disappointed about missing out. Being overlooked is hard to take at any time, but we're talking about every cricketer's dream here – an England tour. To his credit, he copped it sweet and vowed to fight his way back in the best possible manner, by making runs.

[The omission of Jones from the Ashes squad caused controversy in the media, at the pub and around barbecues – especially in his home state, Victoria. He was a key player on the 1989 tour, scoring 566 Test runs at 70.75 with two centuries. Before being eased out during the West Indies series of '92–93, Jones had toured Sri Lanka in 1992 where he topped the Test aggregates with 276 Test runs at 55.20 including a century and two half-centuries. Everyone, including Merv, seemed to think that he'd get the nod for England after being called up for the one-day series in New Zealand.

Mind you, Merv said, there was no talk about England among the players during the New Zealand tour. The topic was put to one side while they got on with the job at hand; they'd concentrate on England later. Jones, who earns his living from cricket, must have felt he was a good chance for a tour berth as he had knocked back the professional's job with English county side Durham. – IC]

I felt for Deano. He's a great batsman and, above all, he's a mate. I also felt for another mate, Tony Dodemaide, who was given a good chance of being picked. Doddy played a few one-dayers in Australia during the summer before being made 12th man for the final two Tests against the West Indies. This led to his selection for the one-day series in New Zealand.

Doddy and I happened to be together when we got the news of the announcement of the touring team. He was driving me around because I'd just had the knee operation and we called in to see John Forbes, Puma's national promotions manager, at his office. Forbesy rang a radio station which was just about to go to air with the official line-up. He put the phone down and said he had some good news and some bad news.

I must admit I was a bit more confident of being selected than in 1989, but you take nothing for granted. You want to hear that you're in. Before Forbesy could say anything, Doddy leaned forward and extended his hand to congratulate me. It was obviously a moment of great disappointment for him, but he didn't let that interfere with his being pleased for someone else.

Sunday 25 April: Somewhere over Australia aboard QF9

[The team is only a few hours out of Melbourne when the tension starts building and the nerves jangle. It is, after all, the ultimate tour and the battle has begun. This is the battle for Five Hundred supremacy! Card games are a popular pastime among sporting teams as they travel around. In this case, the contest was planned to run not simply for the duration of the flight, but for the four months ahead. The combatants, Hughes and Boon versus Zoehrer and Warne. – IC]

This is the big one and I'm nervous. We've got experience on our side, but we're in trouble by Singapore. The scoreboard reads 7–4 in their favour. Perhaps this is a good omen for Warnie's first tour. Heard another good omen for the young blokes just after leaving Melbourne: my AFL team, Footscray, beat Essendon 20.7 (127) to 11.15 (81). Scott West, playing only his fourth game, kicked six goals for Footscray. Go Doggies!

The players are spread out all over the plane, but they wander about and talk during the flight. Boonie, when he's not partnering me at Five Hundred, collects money from the boys for a new ghettoblaster for the rooms. The purchase is made in a duty-free shop at Singapore airport.

Learn that Tugga and Maysie are also doing books about the tour. So, get the camera out and start snapping. [This will give our book a distinct marketing advantage – we've got brilliant photos from Merv 'The Lens' Hughes; they'll be selling their books with colouring pencils! – IC]

After four hours' sleep, the cards resume. A marathon five-hour session sees us make a great comeback. On arrival at Heathrow, Ziggy and Warnie lead by the narrowest of margins, 11–10.

[As always, a Test series between the old enemies Australia and England produced plenty of interest and the tourists were greeted by a huge media posse including four TV crews and a dozen or so press photographers. The Australians looked predictably dapper, having changed back into the business suits after relaxing on the flight in their team tracksuits. Back home, the papers were full of stories about the Australians winning the fashion stakes and sporting a clean-cut image. Obviously, Merv was hiding up the back. – IC]

Collect our gear and head for the coach which will take us around England for the next four months. Full marks to the designer who has put the seats facing each other with tables in between – perfect for card-playing. The table gets a try-out with a few hands on the way to the team hotel, the Westbury.

My first roommate for the tour is Brendon Julian. BJ has done a bit of touring with West Australian teams and the Australian Under-19s, but I don't think it has prepared him for rooming with me. Within an hour, I have stuff everywhere. Tell him that I just want to check that everything has arrived in one piece.

Lunch follows, then 10 of us head off to the gym for a light workout. Later, there is a team meeting at the hotel. Discuss various aspects of the tour such as clothing, training, etc.

Join AB, Babs, Pistol and Marto to wind up the day with a typical English night out at a typical English pub.

Monday 26 April: London

Straight down to business with a training session at the Nursery at Lord's. This is a traditional start to an Australian visit to England and a great thrill for a cricketer whether he's making his first tour (Unit, Cracka, BJ, Marto, Pistol, Slats, Warnie, Junior) or his fourth (AB).

I'm still recovering from the knee operation so my involvement is restricted. Bowling is out of the question, so I walk around the ground a couple of times before jogging a lap. [Big effort! – IC] Finish off the morning with a hit in the nets and some treatment.

The card game continues at lunch. Ziggy and Warnie slip out to a 15–11 lead. After lunch, rain forces training to the indoor nets. Maysie and myself have more treatment.

Back to the Westbury Hotel for a meeting with the team sponsor people and a 90-minute gym session with Hooter, Warnie and Unit. Dinner at an Italian place with Ziggy, Unit, Warnie and team manager Des Rundle. [I wondered how long it would be before Merv mentioned food. It's no secret that he loves a feed and I've got a feeling we'll read plenty about his dining exploits. – IC]

Perhaps the most important development of the day is the formation of two teams within the team. This sort of thing is

16

part of any team sport and helps build team spirit. In this case, we form the Nerds and the Julios. A Nerd needs no explanation while the Julios, the good-looking blokes in the squad, take their name from Julio Iglesias.

The Nerds are: Maysie (c), Heals, Tubby, AB, Me, Tugga, Ziggy, Babsie, Simmo and Pistol.

The Julios are: Hooter, Slats, BJ, Billy, Junior, Unit, Warnie, Cracka and Marto.

Tuesday 27 April: London

Training kicks off at 9 am with a long warm-up followed by a session in the nets. No bowling again for me. It's only day two, but the boys are starting to give me a bit of stick about not bowling. Get some ice and ultrasound treatment on the knee. Go to the gym near the hotel.

Feel like a good Indian feed. London is full of Indian restaurants; the problem is sorting out the good ones from the shockers. Call on Tim May who is an expert. He recommends a 'great little place just around the corner' and gives the directions to BJ and myself. Forty minutes later . . .

Cards update: Boon and Hughes in big trouble after lunchtime game. Zoehrer and Warne break away to a 16–11 lead.

Wednesday 28 April: London

Training at 9 am again. More of the usual knee treatment for me. Ice, ultrasound and differential machine. [I think Merv meant 'inferential' machine, which uses suction caps and electronic impulses to stimulate the recovery of damaged tissue. – IC] Manage to get a hit in the nets.

Off to the Savoy Hotel for the British Sportsman's Club luncheon. Work off lunch with a gym session. Later, meet with a bloke from a sports management group and talk about writing for the Daily Mirror and the possibility of some other promotional work. Team attends MCC dinner at Lord's in evening, then home. A quiet night.

Cards update: Boon and Hughes make sensational comeback on the bus trip from Lord's to the Savoy. Scoreboard now reads 17–14 in favour of Ziggy and Warnie.

Thursday 29 April: London

Up early for a sponsor photo shoot then off to practice at Lord's. More treatment on the knee with the ultrasound and differential machines. Have a bit of a run around, do some fielding and have a hit. Wrapped up the morning with a team photo shoot.

Back to the hotel for a gym session with Hooter until 3.45 pm. Hit the hay for a few hours in the afternoon. A few of the boys play golf while I sleep. [Sleeping runs a very close second to eating as Merv's favourite pastime. – IC]

Wake up and go out for Italian dinner with AB and Ziggy. Popped into a pub for a couple of beers on the way back to the Westbury. Home at 11.30 and discover BJ sound asleep. He's been to see Phantom of the Opera. [And these blokes reckon life on tour is hell! You could have fooled me – lunch at the Savoy, dinner at Lord's, Phantom of the Opera. Where do you apply? – IC]

Friday 30 April: Radlett

Start playing cricket. The first match is against the England Amateur XI. [Isn't that the Test side? – IC] The game is played at Radlett, about 50 minutes out of London. I'm just as keen as England to have a look at some of my new teammates in action. For example, this is the first time I've seen Michael Slater bat. He looks pretty good with 40-odd while Matt Hayden gets 151.

We win fairly easily, knocking them over for 198. Cracka and BJ pick up three wickets each while Billy and Warnie get two each. I'm 12th man for the day and spend most of the time signing autographs, millions of them.

After the game, our hosts turn on the hospitality. A few beers are consumed and a lot of lies are told. Not a bad night. The bus trip home gets dangerous when a few of the boys play at being World Wrestling Federation stars instead of cricketers. [Just as well it wasn't Sumo wrestling! – IC]

Australia 3/292 cc (M. Hayden 151, M. Taylor 53) d. England Amateur XI 198 (W. Holdsworth 3/28, B. Julian 3/60) by 94 runs.

Saturday 1 May: London

Training at Lord's includes yet more treatment for the knee. The frustration is growing. [He was not only frustrated at being unable to bowl for two months, but also worried that the knee mightn't come up. – IC] To take my mind off it, we go to Wembley Stadium in the afternoon to watch the Silk Cut Cup Rugby League final where Wigan beats Widnes in a tough encounter. AB, Tubby, Simmo and Des Rundle watch from a box with the nobs, but the rest of us get good seats and no-one is complaining.

When you spend most of your sporting life out on the playing arena, it's an interesting experience to sit in the crowd for a change. No doubt about it, the Poms are as fanatical about Rugby League as they are about soccer. As for the cricket, well, that appears to be a different story at the moment.

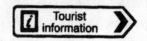

Sunday 2 May: Arundel

Up early for a 7.30 am departure to Arundel, site of the famous Arundel Castle and home of the Duchess of Norfolk. Australian teams traditionally play a tour-opener at Arundel. It's a great setting and a huge crowd always turns out to enjoy the festivities. Today, 15,000 roll up and it would be nice to think they're all here to see us, but the opposition includes one I.T. Botham.

There is a lot of talk about him and David Gower playing in the Test series. Botham makes his bid with 2/29 off 10 overs. One of his scalps is AB, who plays an inside edge on to his stumps. It's 5/68 when AB goes, but Heals and Tugga retrieve the situation.

The boys bowl and field well to defend the total and we win by a couple of runs. There are a few anxious moments, though, as Paul Parker, from Durham, has a red hot go in the last over bowled by Cracka. They need 22 and Parker smashes 6,4,4 before falling lbw.

The two-hour trip home on the bus is the setting for

more exciting action as Babsie and I hit back at cards, recovering from 14–18 down to be 20-all at the close.

Australia 9/203 cc (S. Waugh 59) d. Duchess of Norfolk's XI 196 (M. Waugh 5/32, B. Julian 3/49).

Monday 3 May: London

Game No. 3 on tour is a one-dayer against Middlesex at Lord's. The young guns revel in the opportunity to play at the famous ground with Hayden a ton, and Marto batting really well. Middlesex reply with 174. McDermott, Reiffel and Cracka bowl well, Maysie is steady and Marto completes a memorable day for himself by picking up a couple of handy wickets.

After the game, the boys get done up in their blazers for a reception at the Australian High Commission. Catch up with Ian Maddocks, who has been living in London for the last four years. He's a former Victorian wicket-keeper and we chat about the blokes we played with and against.

Not a bad night, finishing up about 10.30. Back to the Westbury and order room service. [Obviously, not enough to eat at the High Commission! – IC]

Australia 5/243cc (M. Hayden 122, D. Martyn 66) d. Middlesex 174 (D. Martyn 3/41, C. McDermott 3/51) by 69 runs.

Tuesday 4 May: Worcester

Leave London in the morning for the two-hour drive to Worcester, scene of our first three-day game on tour. The cards get a run on the bus, but it's not the big game as Boonie isn't interested. Tubby Taylor takes his place and we beat Ziggy and Warnie easily, 6–3.

After lunch with AB, Unit, Tubby, BJ and Junior, we train at the ground of county side Worcestershire. A good session including a game of touch football between Nerds and Julios. Nerds win easily; Julios obviously worried about ruining their good looks and getting a few hairs out of place.

Go for a curry for dinner with Simmo, Maysie, Slats, Billy and Heals, then on to a pub called the Slug and Lettuce. Have a few beers and play the pinball machines. Home about 11.

Wednesday 5 May: Worcester

So far the weather in England has been sensational and today is no exception. We bat first and make 262. Boonie gets a ton and Tugga 49 not out. By stumps, Worcestershire are 1/14. While all this is going on, I have a couple of net sessions and more treatment on the knee. Off to the gym with Maysie for a burst on the exercise bike and a swim.

As part of the sponsorship deal with XXXX, we are doing some pub appearances during the tour and tonight is the first one. The format is a quiz night with four teams, each captained by an Australian player.

In the first semi-final, Boon's team beats Hayden's. The second semi features AB's team against my team. We win. The final is close, but we just beat Boon's team.

[I later heard that one of the contestants, plucked from the pub crowd, received plenty of attention from a photographer thanks to a short skirt and a low-cut top. Part of the competition involved her – and other contestants – trying to deck out the cricketers in their playing gear in a race against the clock. Can you imagine, for example, this scantily clad young lady fumbling about with Merv's protector? Hilarious stuff, maybe. But not so funny if the young lady has been encouraged, shall we say, by one of the racy tabloids. And even more unfunny if a photo is used entirely out of context. It didn't happen in this case, but that's the sort of nonsense the cricketers – and other high-profile people in England – sometimes run into with the tabloids. – IC]

Thursday 6 May: Worcester

Second day of match against Worcestershire and the bowlers rip through the opposition. Pistol, Cracka and BJ take three wickets each as the home side is bowled out for 90 before lunch. It's a different story in the afternoon as Worcestershire race to 3/300-plus. Graeme Hick smashes 160-odd and gives Warnie a fair bit of stick.

Away from the action, I have a couple of good net sessions. In the second one, bowl for half an hour at three-quarter pace and the knee feels good. More treatment then down to the gym for exercise bike and swim.

The plan is for me to bowl in the next match against Somerset so, to finish the day, it's arranged for me to have a bowl on the centre wicket off my full run. It's only a 10-

minute test, equivalent to sending down about two overs, but this is an important step on the comeback road. Everything goes well and the knee feels good.

[Merv later told me during a late-night phone call that another part of the preparation for his return to the playing field was a heart-to-heart talk with Bob Simpson and Errol Alcott. They discussed his knee, his weight and his future in the game. It sounded like pretty heavy stuff and it also sounded like something I'd heard a few times in the past. He explained that it didn't hurt to go over it again and get things re-focused. He emphasised that a lot of positives came out of their little chat and he resolved to work harder away from the ground. Top of the list of matters for attention was his eating habits. Having said that, Merv wound up our conversation to answer a knock at his hotel room door. In the background, I thought I could hear an English voice saying, 'Room service for Mr Hughes.' – IC]

Friday 7 May: Worcester

Last day of game. Hick continues his onslaught briefly including three sixes off one over from Warnie. One of the shots goes over the entrance gate and into the street, causing the umpires to call for a replacement ball. I'd love to be out there having a hit. I've got an unofficial contest going with Craig McDermott to see who can hit the most sixes on the tour and the short boundaries here are perfect.

Worcestershire declares at 4/458, leaving us 287 to get off 55 overs. The chase is on with Tubby, Unit and Boonie showing the way. With 12 needed off the last over, we get a bit anxious. The target gets down to six off two balls. Not a problem. Tugga only needs one ball and he smashes it for six. An otherwise regulation day for me – warm up, bowl for a while, treatment on knee, down to the gym with Maysie for exercise bike and swim.

Leave for Taunton, venue for the next match against Somerset. Get caught in traffic on the M5 and stop for some food. The coach, which has two videos, is split into two groups for the drive. Down the front we've got the New South Wales and Queensland boys watching the State of Origin Rugby League replay; up the back are the blokes from the Aussie Rules states – Pistol, Maysie, Warnie, Boon, Ziggy, BJ, Marto and myself – watching Wayne's World.

Australia 262 (D. Boon 108) and 5/287 dec. (D. Boon 106, Hayden 96) d. Worcestershire 90 (W. Holdsworth 3/15, P. Reiffel 3/21, B. Julian 3/31) and 4/458 dec. (G. Hick 187) by five wickets.

Saturday 8 May: Taunton

Leave Castle Hotel at 9.15 am for first day of the Somerset match. I'm a little bit toey. My knee feels good but there are always a few doubts when you're coming back after an injury. We win the toss and bat, further delaying the comeback.

The lunch score is 2/166, a fair first session. Slats, playing his first first-class game for Australia, might be a bit toey, too. If he is, he's not showing it. He's 88 not out at lunch. AB claps him off the field, a big wrap.

The run feast continues after lunch with the score reaching 431 despite losing an hour because of bad light and rain. I make 36 runs and £25, thanks to a silly bet with Heals. Silly for him, that is. He offers 20 quid for a six over the long, western boundary and five quid for any six after that. Easy money. Not a problem.

Back to the hotel and over to a wine bar across the road. Sling some of the day's earnings through a fruit machine. A few beers, then home about midnight feeling pretty relaxed and ready to bowl tomorrow.

Sunday 9 May: Taunton

Second day of Somerset game. Only 47 overs bowled because of rain. Billy bowls well and Warnie looks more relaxed. I bowl 15 overs in two spells without taking a wicket, but the most important thing is that the knee feels OK. As for the bowling, I'm either too full or too short and get hit for too many fours. [Nothing unusual! – IC]

Cards come out during the rain delay. We're back to the big one. Ziggy and Warnie shoot to a 25–21 lead after I make some pretty ordinary calls. Babsie Boon is not too happy. Also take the chance to conduct first fines meeting of the tour.

[The three-man fines committee comprised Paul Reiffel (chairman), Michael Slater, and Merv. Fines meetings were held about every two weeks with the committee handing out penalties for anything from lateness to poor dress standards. 'If anyone was late for the bus they were fined 50p per minute for the first 10 minutes and one pound a minute thereafter,' explained Merv. 'Another no-no was wearing leather shoes with a tracksuit. That sort of thing was deplorable and brought the team into disrepute.' The fines went into a team fund used for buying videos, props for practical jokes and an end-of-tour night out. In addition to the fines, a hideous outfit known as the Daktari Suit was 'awarded' to the player who had committed the most embarrassing act or uttered the silliest statement since the previous meeting. Although recipients were mostly seen wearing the Daktari Suit around the team hotel, there were a couple of occasions when it was worn on social outings, much to everyone's amusement. – IC]

Ziggy Zoehrer also introduces the fines meeting to a toy version of Plucka Duck from Channel Nine's 'Hey! Hey! It's Saturday'. Ziggy says Plucka will be in the rooms wherever we're playing and presented to anyone who makes a duck. Cracka, who made a blob against Worcestershire, is the first recipient. He quickly hands it on to Tubby, who made a duck yesterday.

Back to hotel about 7.30 pm and out to a curry house called Raj Poot Tandoori with Maysie, Tubby and Slats. Best one on tour so far. [I'm unsure whether that means the food was good or there was simply lots of it. – IC]

Monday 10 May: Taunton

Last day of game. Somerset declares at overnight score. Have some treatment on the knee while Tubby and Slats push the lead out to 320. There's a bit of a blow-up between AB and Billy after the first over costs 14 runs including three no-balls. Nothing too serious, though.

[Nothing too serious? This was the incident captured by a Channel Seven crew using a directional microphone. All the TV stations ran the Border–McDermott clash and the papers were full of it. Remember how Border, using colourful language, told McDermott he'd be on 'the next plane home' if the fast bowler tested him again? While the media went to town on the subject, it's interesting to read Merv's reaction as 'nothing too serious'. As a fast bowler, he's apparently used to being cranked up by the skipper. – IC]

Go on to win the game with Warnie and Maysie taking four wickets each, but I really struggle with the ball. Some consolation when I claim my first wicket of the tour – Lathwell, caught Zoehrer. I have heaps of work to do. On the positive side, I bat well.

From a team point of view, we are winning games – all five so far, in fact – but we are not playing that well. The batsmen are doing the job, but the bowling and fielding lack intensity.

Australia 431 (M. Slater 122, M. Waugh 68, A. Border 54) and 0/40 d. Somerset 4/151 dec. and 285 (T. May 4/75, S. Warne 4/77) by 35 runs.

Tuesday 11 May: Hove

Travel to Hove for the next match against Sussex. Departure time is 9 am, but a couple of blokes think it's a 9.30 start and are caught running late. [No prizes for guessing one of them is a fast bowler who likes his sleep and has the same initials as Merv Hughes. –IC]

The coach is half-empty anyway as half the team have taken cars so they can play golf on the way to Hove. The on-board entertainment is a couple of videos. Try to catch up on some sleep and miss the first video. Woke up for the second one, Good Morning Vietnam. Get some laughs out of that.

Hotel in Hove is like a rabbit warren with small rooms. The lift is as big as a match box and can take only two people at a time – with no luggage. I've got a new roommate – Cracka Holdsworth. The young quicks - BJ, Cracka and Pistol - will each get a turn with me and also with Billy. The idea is to mix up the younger blokes with the older ones. We'll talk cricket at some stage and hopefully I can pass on a bit of my experience to them. Sleep most of the afternoon and then go to a reception for Australian wine importers.

Out to dinner then home to bed early. Cracka and Marto go out to a nightclub, but they leave after a couple of beers because they're hassled by a few blokes.

Wednesday 12 May: Hove

Start the day by turning on the TV to catch the early morning news. The newsreader has a story about a wild brawl outside a nightclub in Brighton. The report says

30 people were involved and seven have ended up in hospital with stab wounds.

Cracka says, 'Shit! We were there. That's the place. Lucky we came home.'

Walk to the ground for training, but rain interrupts and Simmo takes the opportunity to have a talk to us. He points out we're not playing well and, in particular, that there was a lack of intensity in the Somerset game. He warns us not to get complacent.

Sleep most of the afternoon. Crap TV until 'Scooby Doo' comes on. Go out for dinner with Pistol, Maysie and Billy. [And guess what? Just for a change, they had curry! – IC]

England names their one-day squad: Gooch, Smith, Stewart, Fairbrother, Hick, Thorpe, Lathwell, Caddick, Pringle, Jarvis, Lewis, Cork and Illingworth. [Lathwell, no doubt, was a lucky choice after being Merv's first – and only – victim on tour. – IC]

Thursday 13 May: Hove

[England's one-day squad had been announced, but the tabloids were more interested in cricket stories of a different kind. Merv was the subject of most attention four years ago, but this time it's Shane Warne. At breakfast this day, Warne was greeted by a story in the *Star* with the headline: Cricket's Sexiest Catch. He was described as 'cricket's heart-throb who'll be bowling the maidens over'. The writer gushed on: 'As his awesome body powers down the pitch, those 13½ stones of rippling muscle prompt gasps from female fans. This blond's got balls!' I don't know Warne's reaction, but Merv described the article as a shocker. – IC]

Off to the ground for the first day of the Sussex game. An amazing ground with a slope of about 20 feet from one end to the other. They bat first and make 350-odd. BJ bowls well for five wickets while Pistol also bowls well but without luck. Billy's starting to come good and snares a couple. I also pick up two. I feel OK for the first two spells, but the third is a bit ordinary. Overall, it's starting to come together.

The catching is a highlight of the day. Unit takes two good ones at second slip and gully while AB takes a gem at first slip. There's a huge bath in the dressing room and I jump in for half an hour after play.

Walk back to hotel. Out for dinner with Billy and Tubby. [Something completely different, Indian! – IC]

Friday 14 May: Hove

Second day of Sussex game. Get the usual treatment on the knee while the boys are rattling up 3/306. Rain stops play just after tea. Slats and Unit, who are vying for an opening berth, show their stuff. AB, Marto and Tugga also get among the runs. Choosing the batting line-up for the one-day series starting next Wednesday is not going to be easy.

Meanwhile, back at the betting tent, Ziggy Zoehrer wins friends courtesy of the form guide. He picks out a horse and a syndicate is formed for a plunge at

Ladbroke's. Simmo, AB, Warnie, Tugga and myself join Ziggy in the venture. The money goes on, the horse wins and the plunge is pulled off. [That's if you can call winning £40 a plunge! – IC]

Back to the hotel when play is abandoned. Watch TV and order room service. Go downstairs later and meet Noreen from the Daily Mirror. She's doing a feature article and we chat for about an hour. I'll be interested to see how it turns out. ['Cricket's Unsexiest Catch'? – IC]

Saturday 15 May: Hove

A cold wind is blowing straight up the ground when we arrive for the final day of the Sussex match. The warm-up is called a warm-up, but it doesn't work for me at all. Solution: Go back in to the rooms, fill the bath with steaming hot water and jump in. Babsie, Tubby, Warnie and Junior, who are having the match off, have a better idea. They go to Wembley for the FA Cup final between Arsenal and Sheffield Wednesday.

Out in the middle, Marto and Tugga score hundreds and we declare an hour after lunch at 5/490. Sussex bat again before stumps are drawn early. The cricket match is a draw, but the punters have another win on the horses. [Bookies of the world, you have been warned. Look out for the Ziggy Zyndicate. And look out for a big man with a black moustache and bulging pockets. – IC]

At this stage, apart from the knee, the biggest problem on tour is packing the coffin after each game. [The 'coffin' is the big case that each cricketer puts all his gear in. – IC] No matter how hard you try, things just don't seem to fit. I know everything comes out, but I'm buggered if I can get it back in. Finally work it out and we board the coach for Northampton.

Australia 5/490 (D. Martyn 136, S. Waugh 124, M. Slater 73, M. Hayden 66) v. Sussex 353 (B. Julian 5/63) and 4/92. Match drawn.

Sunday 16 May: Northampton

There was a bundle of goodies waiting for me at reception when we arrived last night. The package contained a bottle of Bailey's, a box of chocolates and a bunch of roses. They're from Sue, for our first wedding anniversary. [The Bailey's and the chocolates, no doubt, were the perfect accompaniment for dinner consumed earlier at Hungry Jack's. – IC]

We're playing a limited-overs match against Northamptonshire today as a lead-up to the Texaco Trophy one-day series. It's another very cold morning and we bowl first on a slow, low wicket. The one-dayers here are 55-over games as opposed to the 50-over affairs at home. Maysie bowls his full quota of 11 and goes for 49, Pistol sends down nine for 35. In contrast, I bowl nine for 52. Funnily enough, I think I bowl OK, but I just seem to get hit as Northants make 2/273.

There's a bit of drama when my knee locks as I'm warming up to bowl the first over after lunch.

[A bit of drama? I think I'd better take over here. I couldn't believe my eyes when I saw this entry, but then I realised that this was typical Merv. Although he is a larger-than-life character who is often accused of going over the top on the field, he is not inclined to talk things up be they good or bad. However, when I quizzed him on the phone about the 'knee lock scare', he revealed his concern. 'I was doing some bending and stretching when it went: Bang! I didn't know what was going on apart from the fact that I couldn't straighten my leg because the knee was locked. So I called out to AB that I had a bit of a problem and wouldn't be able to bowl.' Nothing like this had ever happened to Merv before, not even during the rough and tumble of his 95 games of Australian Rules football with Werribee. He admitted, 'For a moment, I feared the worst and the tour flashed before my eyes. It could have been all over there and then.'

'Just think what that would have meant,' I said. 'No more Tests, no more Ashes, no more Indian dinners!' At this point, Merv suggested how I could better occupy my time rather than ringing him. Anyway, back to the story. Merv said that as soon as the knee locked, he came straight off the ground to see Errol Alcott, who got things moving again. However, he didn't want to take any chances and it was arranged that Merv would see a specialist.

Putting the team first, Merv waited until tea when the score had reached 0/120 off 25 overs before hopping in the car to drive with Alcott to Cambridge to see the specialist. After the appointment, the pair headed back north to rejoin the team which had moved onto Manchester after the Northants game.

Worried that the book project could be scuttled by Merv's knee collapsing, not to mention the defence of the Ashes, I rang Manchester to hear the news. The first thing I learned was that Merv had yet another new roommate, his Victorian teammate Paul Reiffel, whose cricketing education was being rounded out. His first lesson was answering the phone, and the second was ordering room service. Anyway, Merv came on the line and announced that his knee was 'not a problem'. The specialist thought the locked knee was probably caused by a bit of roughage getting caught on the patella tendon. Merv said, 'The other good news is that there's a little soreness but no swelling. The soreness can probably be explained by the fact that I've played two three-day games and a one-dayer in a row after a period of doing virtually nothing. All this means I can keep going at full pace.' It was the most buoyant Merv had sounded since leaving Australia, a good sign for the coming one-day series. – IC]

Australia 2/183 (M. Taylor 89 not out, M. Waugh 74) lost to Northamptonshire 2/273 on run rate.

2 The One-Day Clean Sweep

WINNING Test matches is what cricket is all about, so the Australians were not overly concerned when they lost the one-day series in 1989. Well, that was their story, but really they don't like to lose any match.

Going into the one-day series this time there was a resolve to establish an early supremacy over England. And with the Australian batsmen in good form, there was pressure on for spots in the Test line-up. For Merv, there was a different kind of pressure as he prepared to put his knee to the test.

Monday 17 May: Manchester

Leave for ground at 9 am. Not there long as Simmo calls off training because of the cold, wet conditions. Back to the hotel. Make a few phone calls. Ring FOX-FM [A Melbourne radio station on which Merv appears regularly.] Go for a walk around Manchester with Billy, Marto, Slats, Heals and BJ. The five of us have haircuts and I also have a shave – the perfect preparation for a big game.

This probably sounds like a pretty boring day, but you need one every now and then when you're on a long tour. It's a chance to relax and do some normal things. There's a cinema over the road from the hotel which also helps pass the time. Go to see Indecent Proposal *with Billy, Warnie and BJ.*

Get another movie fix with Cape Fear *on the hotel video. Go downstairs for a drink and then back to room. Watch* Cape Fear *again. [Is this a possible after-cricket career for Merv? Taking over from Bill Collins as a TV movie host? – IC]*

Tuesday 18 May: Manchester

Yesterday's rest and relaxation seems to have worked wonders as this morning's training session sparkles. With the first big game on tomorrow, the boys slip up a notch and the intensity is sustained for three hours. Get the full treatment on the knee – ice, ultrasound and differential.

Back to hotel and sit around for a while. Ring Sue who has some good news – she's coming over on 17 June. Off to the movies again with Billy and Warnie to see Accidental Hero. *Return to hotel and discover that a few people have rung while we've been at the movies. Among the callers is Darren 'Chuck' Berry, the Victorian wicket-keeper who is over here playing cricket. Another caller is Marty Peacock, one of my old football coaches. He's over here on holidays. It doesn't matter where you go in the world, you always manage to run in to someone you've met through sport.*

The build-up for tomorrow starts with a team meeting over dinner. Our XII is named: Border (c), Taylor (vc), Boon, Hayden, Healy, Hughes, McDermott, Martyn, May, Reiffel, M. Waugh, S. Waugh. I fancy Unit will be 12th man and Tubby and Junior will open. We'll see in the morning. [Apart from naming the Australian team, the meeting also took a close look at the likely England team, but Merv was tight-

MERV'S SNAPS

The scene in my room half an hour after arriving in London.

First game on tour. Hayden and Slater go out to open against the England Amateur XI at Radlett.

Three of the game's greats at Arundel — Ian Botham, AB and Joel Garner.

My Victorian team-mates Warnie and Pistol enjoy the atmosphere at Arundel.

Worcester — does this look a good place to play cricket or what? Boonie is the batsman on strike, Hayden backing up.

Worcester — Maysie and Pistol get down to the business of autographing a few dozen bats.

Tugga rugs up against the cold weather at Hove, Sussex.

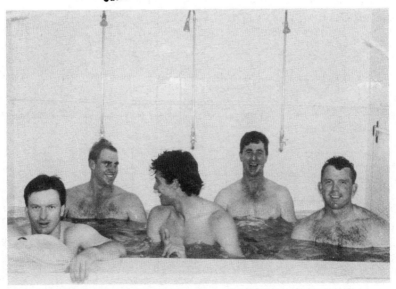

Sussex again. We're in the bath to warm up after play. From left: Tugga, Unit, BJ, Maysie and I forget this bloke's name (Only joking! It's Billy before he got crook and went home).

AB rings his bookmaker to get the odds after we win the first one-day international. The other blokes are Keith Fletcher (England manager) and South Australia's Peter Sleep.

The Nerds dressed and ready to go ten-pin bowling.

Chief nerds Tugga and Maysie. Say no more.

Welcome to Test cricket, BJ. Plucka was passed on to him after he made a duck in the first innings of the first Test at Old Trafford.

Cooling down Heals's bat after he blazes a ton in our second innings at Old Trafford.

Come in spinners. Maysie and Peter Such talk about the art of bowling offies during the first Test.

Mike Gatting still looks stunned as Warnie (in cap) talks him through *that* ball in the first Test.

All the boys with their ears on at Bristol.

lipped about what was discussed. One can only assume that his contribution was promising to bowl fast at everyone. – IC]

Back in room at 10 pm and watch An Officer and a Gentleman on TV.

Wednesday 19 May: Manchester (First One-Day International)

There is a good, positive feeling among the team as we head off to Old Trafford at 9 am. I'm a bit surprised when AB announces Unit will open with Tubby, and Marto is 12th man. I thought Junior might open with Marto in the middle order and Unit as 12th. Glad I'm not a selector.

The next surprise is that Gooch wins the toss and sends us in. Some experts believe that the early conditions will favour the England seamers, but runs on the board are always very hard to beat. Any fears about the wicket or weather conditions disappear as Tubby and Unit put on 60 for the first wicket. Junior comes in and makes a rapid 56 and we're steaming along at 1/168. A couple of quick wickets fall and it's 3/173 off 41 overs.

The score is hoisted to 9/258 thanks to quickfire innings from Tugga and Heals. A day out for me as I score 20 off 13 balls at the finish including a six off Pringle.

[I was listening in bed at this stage and heard the BBC radio commentators going on and on about this massive blow struck by Hughes. I later mentioned it to Merv who explained that, 'When you're 17 stone with a 3½lb bat in your hands and it comes off the middle, there's a good chance it'll go a long way. Especially if you close your eyes first.' A 3½lb bat, by the way, is more like a tree trunk than a cricket bat. – IC]

England bats and are in early trouble at 3/44. Billy bowls really well picking up Gooch and Smith, who falls to a brilliant one-handed caught and bowled. Hick and Fairbrother stage a revival putting on 120-odd. Hick gives Pistol a bit of stick, but Pistol has the last laugh when he claims his wicket at a crucial time.

The pendulum swings back our way as a couple more quick wickets fall. That puts the brakes on the run flow along with three tight overs from Billy which cost just eight runs. However, England is in with a chance as six runs are required off the last over.

[And who is the man charged with the responsibility of bowling this all-important final over? Good old Swervin! I woke up in time to see this gripping finish on TV. Actually, the baby woke up first and I was more than happy to get up and nurse her for a while. I just had to make sure she wasn't looking at the screen when the cameras went for a close-up on Merv. The last two batsmen – Richard Illingworth and Andy Caddick – were at the crease and must have given themselves a chance to get the runs. Merv, meanwhile, was simply concerned with seeing that they didn't. Caddick played a copybook off drive which looked like going for four, but Tim May pulled off a copybook diving save. Merv described it more as a case of the ball hitting May. In the pressure-cooker atmosphere, with two balls remaining, the batsman tried for a second run that patently wasn't there and Caddick was run out. Australia had won and, more importantly, the baby was asleep. – IC]

We win by four runs and Billy is named Man of the Match with figures of 11-2-38-3. I finish with 1/40 off 9.5 overs and feel good. The knee is no problem and I reckon I'm not far away from reaching top gear. The first Test is only two weeks away so I'm coming good at the right time.

I know we've come here to do more than just win a one-day match, but a win's a win. A few celebratory beers are in order. Then it's back to the hotel for dinner and a few more beers. Go to bed about 1 am thinking a good day has been had by all. [What? No in-house video? – IC]

Australia 9/258 (M. Taylor 79, M. Waugh 56) d. England 254 (G. Hick 85, N. Fairbrother 59; C. McDermott 3/38, S. Waugh 3/53) by four runs. Man of the Match: Craig McDermott.

Thursday 20 May: Birmingham

Leave Manchester for Birmingham at 10 am with Pistol. Go by car for a change. Check in to hotel and go out for some lunch – fish and chips. Back to room and watch TV before heading off to practice at 2.30. It's a bit wet, but we manage to train for a while and get the feel of the Edgbaston ground for the second one-day international being played here tomorrow.

Back to the hotel and ring Bill Lawry who is over here in his role as a commentator on Channel Nine. Bill also is

cricket manager for the Victorian Cricket Association and we
have a chat about the state of affairs in Victoria for about an
hour. [Victoria had a disappointing season last summer
and Bill is looking for improvement so he can say, 'It's all
happening here!' – IC].

Back to the room (sharing with Pistol again) and watch
more TV. Go out to a pub around the corner and play
pinball with Marto and Cracka. Get some fish and chips for
tea. Prepare for tomorrow's match by watching a replay of the
FA Cup final on TV.

Friday 21 May: Birmingham (Second One-Day International)

Wake up to a cold, overcast day and head to the ground at
9 am. Discover the ground is wet, but play starts on time
despite everything. The conditions influence AB's
decision when he wins the toss and sends England in to
bat. They've made one change bringing in Dominic Cork

for Richard Illingworth. Billy fires up early again and claims Stewart and Gooch. Pistol chips in to have Hick caught behind by Heals, a nice comeback after the events of two days ago.

Just as things seem to be going OK for us, along comes Robin Smith to play the best one-day innings I've ever seen. For the first few overs, Smith gives no clues that he is about to produce a memorable display until, suddenly, he explodes. Billy manages to keep control (11-1-29-3) along with Maysie (11-0-45-0), but the rest of us take a hammering. Not only does he hit the ball amazingly hard and often, but he seems to miss the field every time. At the end of 55 overs, the England score is 5/277 with Smith unbeaten on 167 off 163 balls.

[Unlike Merv who saw this virtuoso performance up close, I saw only the last over. I was on my way to an after-dinner speaking engagement and heard the start of the England innings on the car radio. As I got out of the car, Gooch fell to McDermott and I was able to relay the news to the dinner audience who roared with delight. Back in the car before midnight, I turned on the radio to hear the BBC's Jonathon Agnew saying, 'and the score moves on to 154'. I thought the Australians had done remarkably well to restrict England to such a small total. As Agnew continued, I discovered that he was talking about one player – Smith – and not the team total! I arrived home in time to catch the last over and heard the applause handed out to Smith. I felt sorry for him that he wasn't walking off the MCG so that he could have received a longer ovation.

Having missed all but the last over, I mused over the following statistics of Smith's innings, the fifth highest in one-day internationals: He went from 100 to 150 off 20 balls in 20 minutes; he scored 116 off 70 balls after lunch; his partnership with Thorpe was worth 142, of which Thorpe contributed 36. All up, Smith hit 18 fours and three 6s. – IC]

We start the chase steadily with Tubby and Unit putting on 30-odd. Junior and Boon put on a few, but Boon gets out last ball before tea. A great partnership between Junior and AB puts the game in our hands and we win by six wickets.

[Merv's account sounds simple and that's very much how the Australians play one-day cricket when chasing a big total. They aim to get away to a solid start, keep the scoreboard ticking over and make sure they've got wickets in hand. When a lot of people would have expected them to be shell-shocked or demoralised by the Smith onslaught, the experienced Aussies remained calm and calculating in the dressing room. 'We always felt we could win,' Merv revealed later. 'The wicket had plenty of runs in it and the boundaries were short.' – IC]

You can't beat that winning feeling and we've not only won today's game but also the Texaco series. Sit in the rooms for a couple of hours to enjoy the spoils and a few beers. Hit the town for some more celebrations then to bed about 1.30 am. A good day had by all.

Australia 4/280 (M. Waugh 113, A. Border 86 not out) d. England 5/277 (R. Smith 167 not out; C. McDermott 3/29) by 6 wickets. Man of the Match: R. Smith.

Saturday 22 May: London

The previous good day is ruined by a shocking morning. The coach is scheduled to leave for London at 11 am, allowing us the chance to sleep in. However, roadworks start outside the hotel and we're awake very early. Jack-hammers are going full-bore at 7.30 am – on the road and in my head.

Try to catch up on lost sleep on the two-hour drive to London, but the movie Fletch grabs my attention. Play some cards, too. Boonie and myself make something of a comeback. Score now stands at 27–24 in favour of Zoehrer and Warne.

Relax in room at hotel. Receive a fax from the VCA about Carlton and United Breweries sponsoring Victorian cricket for the next five years.

[This meant Merv would be changing brands from XXXX to CUB on his return from England. Meanwhile, the wearing of the XXXX logo on the players' clothes provoked an uproar when they were seen during the one-day series. Most people thought the logos were being worn only during the county games and were shocked to learn that jumpers and shirts would carry the logos for the one-dayers and the Tests. Merv acknowledged that the purists might be offended, but asked them to consider the fact that cricket is a business competing with many other sports and forms of entertainment. 'I play cricket for a living,' he said, 'and if sponsorship money goes toward paying my wages, then I'm happy to wear the sponsor's logo.' – IC]

Training at 3 pm is optional, but only four players don't turn up. Back from training at 6 pm and go out for dinner with Ziggy, BJ, Slats and Junior. Tonight's choice is Mexican and it's good, but the after-effects do not make me popular with Pistol when I return to our room.

Sunday 23 May: Lord's (Third One-Day International)

The Texaco series is in the bag, but the boys are keen to make it a 3–0 clean sweep. It's a perfect day at Lord's and both sides have made two changes. Marto gets a chance with AB taking a rest while BJ comes in for Pistol. England brings in Reeve and Illingworth for Lewis and Pringle.

Acting captain Tubby makes a solid 57, but England keeps it fairly tight until Boonie and Marto pick up the pace at the end. Marto gets 51 not out off 43 balls as the total reaches 5/230. I miss out on a hit for the second game in a row. However, I think the 20 runs I scored in my one and only innings beats my best series total.

England gets off to a good start with Gooch and Stewart putting on 96 for the first wicket. Billy picked up Gooch cheaply in the first two games, but he gets going this time. Finally, he sweeps Maysie and I take the catch. [Merv later described the catch as a blinder and claimed the sun was in his eyes. Truth is, it was a regulation catch hit straight down his throat at backward square leg. – IC]

The young blokes provide a couple of highlights. One is BJ, who struggles in the early stages with his first three overs costing 27 runs. He comes back to take 3/23 off eight overs in his second spell and wins the Man of the Match award.

The other highlight comes from Unit who takes a great catch to get rid of Jarvis. [That was the sensational one-hander he plucked out of the air while flinging himself backwards in the outfield. A friend sitting at the opposite end of the ground to the Channel Nine commentary box said he could hear Bill Lawry screaming 'Yeeesssss! Got him! What a catch! That's the best catch I've ever seen! A classic catch, for sure!' – IC] England lose their last seven wickets for 53 runs off nine overs and fall 19 short with 11 balls remaining.

[For the second time in three games, Merv was bowling when the last wicket fell. This put him in the perfect position to grab a souvenir stump or, in this case, two. When I asked him if he was getting greedy, Merv said he had given one to Brendon Julian. 'He was moping around in the dressing room, so I gave one to him to go with his Man of the Match award.'

Merv's previous souvenirs are labelled and stored in a cupboard at home. 'When Sue and I get settled in a bigger house, I'll put them on display,' he said. And before we finished talking about the stumps, Merv had a tip for young players – don't take the stumps which house the stump-cam at each end. Channel Nine likes to hang on to them and they don't muck about when one goes missing. Someone watches a replay to see which player has grabbed it, then a technician goes in to the dressing room and asks for it back. One night in Sydney, Merv grabbed the stump-cam by mistake and the Nine crew didn't know who had it. 'A bloke came in with a special device which he pointed at the players' coffins,' he said. 'It was a bit like one of those metal detectors at the airport. When the thing started beeping at my coffin, he knew he'd found the stump-cam.' – IC]

Australia 5/230 (D. Boon 73, M. Taylor 57, D. Martyn 51 not out; A. Caddick 3/39) d. England 211 (A. Stewart 74; B. Julian 3/50) by 19 runs. Man of the Match: B. Julian.

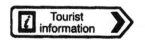

Monday 24 May: London

*You beauty, a day off! Take the laundry downstairs at 8.30
am. Go straight back to bed. I think I deserve a rest after three
hard-fought one-dayers in five days, not to mention the
celebrating. Last night's post-match events included a few
beers in the rooms and a few more at the Regent Hotel with
Ian 'Molly' Meldrum. [Molly is a cricket fanatic and made
two separate trips to England during the series to catch
the action. He also loves a party. If he hasn't got one to go to,
he throws one himself. Every summer he hosts a now-
legendary party for the team after one of the day-nighters at
the MCG. – IC]*

*Get up around lunch time and head out to a cafe with BJ
and Unit. A big golf afternoon is arranged and about a
dozen are playing. Tubby, Warnie and myself play a skins
game with each hole worth a quid. After 18 holes, Warnie
has nine, Tubby eight and me one. No wonder I've always
said golf is an impossible sport. [And no wonder AB once
described Merv as 'the worst golfer he had ever seen in his
life'. – IC]*

*Scrape together enough money for dinner at a rib place
near Sloane Square. Not bad.*

Tuesday 25 May: London

*Back to the three-day county games as we take on Surrey at
the Oval. I get a rest, but the boys are sticking together
whether they're playing or not. We bat first and declare at
9/378 about an hour after tea. West Indian Joey Benjamin,
who played with Prahran in the VCA district competition last*

summer, takes a couple of early wickets. Junior and Marto come together for a 237-run partnership. Junior is on fire [178 off 174 balls including eight 6s.] while Marto makes 80-odd.

My day consists of a game of Monopoly and five laps of the ground when play is stopped by bad light. Hard to say which takes more out of me. For the record, the Monopoly game is played between Slats, Unit and myself. I'm bankrupt and out of business pretty quickly. Monopoly is a bit like golf really . . .

Back to the hotel and then head out to a place called Gaylord's for dinner with Pistol, Maysie, Tubby, Slats, Junior, Heals and BJ. [Sounds English, what, but the food is Indian. – IC] Work off the meal by watching an action-packed Steven Segal movie called Marked For Death.

Wednesday 26 May: London

Surrey bowled out for 231 on the second day. Cracka and Pistol take a couple of wickets while Warnie picks up three. By stumps, batting a second time, we're 2/152.

[For Warne, this was a perfect tune-up for the first Test starting a week later. The mauling at the hands of Hick was well behind him and he was set to play a key role in the series. I asked Merv to get the odds from Ladbroke's about Warne taking more than 20 wickets in the Tests. – IC]

For me, today's activity is a bit more strenuous than yesterday's as I go to the gym with Maysie, Tugga and Heals. Work up an appetite for a Mexican feed. Dine with

Slats, BJ, Ziggy and Maysie at a place called Break for the Border. [Named after the skipper? – IC] Back in the room, manage to upset Pistol again with the after-effects of eating Mexican.

Thursday 27 May: London

Last day of Surrey game. Do warm-ups with the team, then watch till lunch. We bat on briefly before declaring with a lead of 318. By lunch, Surrey has lost two wickets and the boys are on the way to another win. [For the Australians, there was plenty of incentive to win the county games. The tour sponsor had offered a $100,000-plus bonus if Australia could win 10 of its 14 first-class matches against county teams. – IC]

Heals, Tugga, Maysie and myself head off for a game of golf. Maysie is giving directions again and we get lost. Tugga and I pair up against Heals and Maysie. The stakes are higher than Monday's skins game when we played for a quid a hole: today's losers have to shout at McDonald's on the way back to the hotel. Tugga and I get beaten and the burgers are on us.

Greeted back at the hotel with the news that the boys have beaten Surrey. Bowled them out for 144 with Warnie taking four wickets. Ziggy gets himself into the record books alongside Wally Grout for the most dismissals in an innings by an Australian wicket-keeper. He snares eight – six catches and two stumpings.

Out for dinner to a new place called Planet Hollywood which is owned by Arnold Schwarzenegger, Sylvester Stallone and Bruce Willis. A bit to eat, a bit to drink, a good night with most of the team in attendance.

Australia 9/378 (M. Waugh 178, D. Martyn 84) and 4/171 (M. Taylor 80, M. Slater 50) d. Surrey 231 (S. Warne 3/68) and 144 (S. Warne 4/38, B. Julian 3/30) by 174 runs.

Friday 28 May: Leicester

Off to Leicester for another three-day game, the last before the first Test at Old Trafford. Sleep all afternoon and get up about 6.30 pm. Meet Tugga in the bar and head for Hinkley, a nearby town which has a McDonald's. Drop in to the Bounty Hotel for a few drinks, then head back to our hotel. Take a wrong turn somewhere and a 15-minute trip home takes 45. [Which just goes to show you can get lost without Tim May. – IC]

Watch a couple of movies before going to sleep. Tonight's offerings are Predator 2 *and* American Ninja.

Saturday 29 May: Leicester

We win toss and bat on first day of the match against Leicestershire. Bat all day for 3/323 with Boonie getting 123 and Slats 91. He's a real chance for the first Test. AB and Tugga warm up with 40-odd not out each. Run four laps with Heals and Billy after stumps. Do some catching practice, too.

Some loudmouths give us a hard time while we're

going to the team bus. [Merv doesn't mind a bit of playful banter with the fans from time to time, but there are occasions such as this which are intolerable. Merv – and the rest of the team – are expected to grin and bear it because the minute they say something back, it'll be all over the papers. You know, 'Aussie Cricketers Clash With Fans!' I reckon the best way to deal with these loudmouths would be to make them face an over of short-pitched stuff on a green top – without helmets and boxes. – IC]

Back to the hotel for in-house movie viewing. Tonight's double: *Repossessed* and *Boyz 'n the Hood*.

Sunday 30 May: Leicester

Not much of a day for cricket – overcast, cold, windy. We declare at the overnight score and spend most of the time until tea dodging showers. Unit drops both openers in slips off my bowling. [This indiscretion is believed to have cost Hayden a couple of Big Macs and a large fries! – IC] Weather clears up after tea and we play the full session. Maysie and Warnie take three wickets each and Leicestershire is 7/168 at stumps.

Have some treatment on neck and shoulders after play and then jump on the bus back to the hotel. No sign of our mates from yesterday. Another quiet night watching television.

Monday 31 May: Leicester

Last day of the Leicestershire game starts with the home side declaring at the overnight score. We bat for an hour, then declare at 4/88 of which Slats gets 50 not out. Batting a second time, Leicestershire is knocked over for 146 with Warnie and Maysie taking another three wickets each. Billy gets two, BJ one and there is a run out. My contribution for the match is five runs, no wickets and two dropped catches.

Head off to Manchester after the game. Very happy when the bus stops at McDonald's on the way. A few beers on the bus and then a few more after booking in at the hotel. Spirit among the boys is high, a good sign for the first Test. Rooming again with Cracka. [Reiffel, not coping well with the after-effects of Merv's Mexican dinners, is rumoured to have asked management for a switch. – IC]

Australia 3/323 dec. (D. Boon 123, M. Slater 91) and 4/88 dec.(M. Slater 50) d. Leicestershire 7/168 dec. (S. Warne 3/31, T. May 3/62) and 146 (S. Warne 3/27, T. May 3/39) by 97 runs.

Tuesday 1 June: Manchester

Leave hotel for training at Old Trafford. Train for 90 minutes before rain comes. Steady rain for the last few days has seen water soak through the covers on to the centre wicket square. Could be very interesting on Thursday. Do a photo shoot at the ground for razor blades with Graham Gooch. They dress us up in old English gear.

Go in to town with BJ and Slats for a look around, then back to the hotel for a sleep. I like to get plenty of sleep before a Test match. [So do I, especially when I've got to sit up until 3 am watching it on television. – IC]

Get out of bed in late afternoon and head for the 10-pin bowling alley for the second challenge between the Nerds and Julios. Maysie leads the Nerds line-up of Tugga, Simmo, Ziggy, Heals and myself. The Julios – Slats, Cracka, Billy, BJ, Unit and Junior – win by about 10 pins.

Stick around the bowling alley after the big clash and play pinball with Cracka. Walk to a hotel where a barbecue is being held for the Australian team. Chat to a few people then head back to my room. Watch Scanner on in-house video.

Wednesday 2 June: Manchester

Leave for training at 10 am. Get to ground and find it's too wet for nets, so a game of touch rugby is organised. The result is a four-all draw – what a game! Finish off with fielding practice then head back to hotel. Order room service lunch and watch Patriot Games, then sleep for a couple of hours. Up at 6 pm and downstairs for dinner and a team meeting.

[Among the tactics discussed was a plan which involved the fast bowlers Hughes and McDermott giving plenty of short stuff to Graeme Hick. Merv was once again tight-lipped about the ploy, but Allan Border later confirmed it. 'Bowling short is going to be our game plan for him this series,' Border said. 'We perceive it as an area we can attack. He is too dangerous a player for us not to try and exploit it.' – IC]

After dinner, go for one drink in the bar and then head upstairs to relax. Watch TV and an in-house movie called The Public Eye starring Joe Pesci from Lethal Weapon. Not a bad show.

[I don't know how Merv could have an opinion about this movie because I phoned him and interrupted his viewing. Actually, Merv's roommate Wayne Holdsworth answered the phone. I asked him how he was enjoying his first Ashes tour. 'It's great – I'm a net bowler!' he said, referring to his seeing more of the action in the nets than on the playing field. The purpose of my call was to wish Merv well for the Test and to compare our teams. Over lunch before he left for England, Merv had said he wanted to see if I knew anything about Test cricket. So, I went for Taylor, Slater, Boon, M. Waugh, Border, S. Waugh, Healy, Julian, Hughes, Warne, McDermott and May. I thought May would be 12th man because of the wet conditions and the likelihood of a seamers' track. Tuning into Channel Nine a few hours later, I was pleased to see that the selectors agreed with me. Merv, by the way, missed on Julian and Mark Waugh, opting for Reiffel and Martyn. Understandable, I thought, he's too close to the action.

I asked him about his preparation. 'It's been good,' he said, 'the knee's fine and I've been looking after myself. I'm on a special diet.' I asked him if it was working. 'Yes . . . and no,' he replied. As for the team, he felt they were 'going along nicely' but warned that a repeat of 1989 was not a mere formality. 'In '89, we were underdogs and there wasn't as much pressure on us,' Merv said. 'This time, everyone thinks that England is no good and all we've got to do is turn up and play. It's not as easy as that. They've got some very good players in their side and they should not be under-estimated. That's not to say we're not confident, but there's still a job to do.' – IC]

3 Old Trafford, New Star

AND so we came to the first Test at Old Trafford. The build-up was over and the tourists were in good form, particularly the batsmen. As for the bowlers, Shane Warne was promising to inject a special brand of excitement into the Tests with his leg spin, and Merv, well, his troublesome knee had finally come good. The team was winning the county games, that form had continued in the one-day series and the Texaco Trophy was engraved with the letters A U S T R A L I A. The Aussies, of course, already held the main prize – the Ashes – and they were not thinking of relaxing their grip on the famous little urn. Their sights were set and no-one was more focused than Mervyn Gregory Hughes.

For the next five days, Merv's diary revealed that life as one of the spearheads of Australia's bowling attack was very much 'get up, go to ground, play cricket, go home, have dinner, go to bed'. With his thoughts concentrated on winning the Test, Merv appeared to have little time for details or asides. But, frankly, I didn't expect anything else. Anyone looking for fun and games during a Test is way off beam. As Merv himself said, there was a job to do. What follows is Merv's account of that job over the five days of the first Test. After each day, by way of comparison, is my version of events from 20,000 kms away.

Thursday 3 June: Old Trafford

England wins toss and sends us in. Pitch looks as though it would do heaps. Off to a good start with Slats 50-odd and Tubby 120-odd. They put on over 100 for the opening partnership. At one stage, we're 1/170. End up 5/250-odd with AB and Heals not out. For England, spin does the damage with Such taking three. He's a bit of a surprise packet but Caddick is not as potent as we expected.

After match, go into bar. Catch up with a few people including Chuck and Flem [Victorian teammates Darren Berry and Damien Fleming]. Back to room about 8 pm, watch some TV. Ring FOX. Have room service then watch Cape Fear on in-house video.

Thursday 3 June: Melbourne

Like Merv and his knee, I had a problem in the lead-up to the first Test – an aching wisdom tooth. However, unlike Merv, who had knee surgery well before the Test, I chose this day for the removal of the offending tooth. Fortunately, by nightfall, my mouth and face felt almost back to normal and I sat down to watch the action on TV.

Merv had painted a gloomy picture the previous night, but the scene looked terrific when Channel Nine crossed to Old Trafford. Taylor and Slater looked terrific, too, as they guided Australia safely to lunch without loss. Richie Benaud suspected that the wicket was full of gremlins and, indicating that Allan Border held the same opinion, made a point of telling viewers that the skipper had stood to applaud the opening pair as they walked off for lunch. Fine observation that.

During the lunch break, I set up a portable TV on a chair in the corner of the bedroom so I could go to bed and watch the rest of the day's play. As an experienced Ashes follower, I also had a radio within reach for garnering opinions from the BBC experts during TV commercial breaks. I was going nicely for a while, cruising along with Taylor as he approached his century, until disaster struck – I fell asleep.

Friday 4 June: Old Trafford

We lose five wickets in morning session. England get off to a good start with Gooch and Atherton. Then Warnie takes three wickets – Gatting, Smith and Gooch – to swing the game our way. The ball that gets Gatting is a gem. I'm fielding at backward square, so I can't see much but the boys are very excited. Run into the huddle and ask Warnie, 'What happened? Did it turn much?'

At stumps, England 8/202 with Caddick and Such at the wicket.

Back to hotel. Few beers downstairs, then up to room. Ring FOX. Have room service. Watch Cape Fear. Quiet night.

After seeing England bat today, I feel we can still improve. England earned three wickets while we got all but Hick and Gooch with good balls. We got lucky with Hick when he hit a half-tracker off me to AB at point, and Gooch, who was caught at mid-on by BJ off a full toss from Warnie.

Friday 4 June: Melbourne

When I awoke this morning, the TV and radio were both still going, but the cricket was well and truly finished. During the day, I bumped into several people who admitted to falling asleep last night. Everyone agreed that three one-dayers were insufficient preparation for the serious all-night Test viewer. Being in Victoria, there was also plenty of criticism aimed at the Waugh twins. Mark had made six and Steve three, in Australia's first-day score of 5/242. 'I reckon Deano would have made more than nine on his own,' a friend observed.

That evening, I settled down in front of the TV and saw Peter Such spin his way through the tail, leaving Australia all out for 289. The biggest disappointment was seeing Merv fall for just two runs after only 10 minutes at the crease. After hearing tales of his big hitting in the county games, I was hopeful of seeing him take the long handle to Such. [Such is life. – MH]

Merv provided some joy with the ball, however, having Atherton caught behind by Healy to end a 71-run opening partnership with Gooch. He also provided some entertainment when he appeared to have a few words to say to Atherton as he departed the crease. Richie Benaud suggested that Merv was 'inquiring about Atherton's health and, perhaps, his parents'. I later asked Merv about the incident and he claimed it was nothing more than a long-winded appeal . . .

Content with the knowledge that Merv had made the breakthrough, I turned off the TV and went to bed. The radio, of course, was still going quietly on the bedside table. Turning off the TV, though, was a stupid act. Why? Because I missed seeing Shane Warne's 'ball of the century' which dismissed Mike Gatting. I certainly heard all about it from the BBC commentary team on the radio.

Saturday 5 June: Old Trafford

Cracka, Maysie, Marto, Unit, Pistol and Ziggy go down to the ground early for nets. Warnie picks up Caddick and I get Tufnell to end up with four wickets each. BJ gets two. Billy bowls well without taking a wicket. That's another good sign as Billy won't go wicketless in too many innings in Test matches.

Lead by 79, but in trouble early in second innings with Tubby out for nine and Slats for 20-odd. Boon and Junior put on 100 plus before Junior gets out for 64. Boon gets 85 not out, AB 29 not out. We have lead of 300 with seven wickets in hand.

Back to hotel. Have a couple of beers in bar then go out for a couple with Cracka and Marto. Pub shuts at 11, so grab a pizza and catch a taxi home.

Saturday 5 June: Melbourne

I rang a friend early in the morning to arrange meeting him at the football at the MCG that afternoon. The first thing he said was, 'Did you see Warne's delivery that got Gatting last night?' My friend then went into an excited description like those I'd heard from the BBC team last night. 'And would you believe,' he said, 'it was his first ball of the day?'

My colleagues from the Coodabeen Champions were also raving on about the Warne delivery when I arrived at the 3AW studios to present our Saturday morning football show. Victoria was playing South Australia in a big State of Origin football match at the MCG that day, but no-one wanted to talk football. The only topic for discussion was Warne's delivery.

At the MCG, I saw an amazing thing. Groups of football fans were turning their backs on the cream of Victoria's and South Australia's Aussie Rules stars to gather at TV monitors tuned to Sky Channel. Between races, Sky was showing highlights of the previous night's cricket. Everyone was glued to the screens, waiting for a glimpse of the Warne wizardry.

Finally, it came on. It dipped, it bit, it spun, it beat the bat and it hit the top of the off stump. It was brilliant, stunning, exhilirating. No wonder everyone was making a fuss about it. Out on the MCG, another sportsman hailed for freakish feats kicked a sensational goal for Victoria at the very moment Gatting's wicket was broken. Shane Warne, on replay, had upstaged a 'live' Gary Ablett.

Sunday 6 June: Old Trafford

Cracka, Maysie, Marto, Unit, Pistol and Ziggy have early training session again. We lose AB and Boon for 31 and 93 in first half-hour of play. Then Tugga and Heals bat really well putting on 180. We declare half an hour before tea with a lead of 512.

Atherton and Gooch again start well until Warnie gets Atherton caught at slip by Tubby. Then Gatting and Gooch put on 50-odd before I bowl Gatting with the last ball of the day.

Ice up both knees in rooms. Back to hotel. Watch Raising Cain with Cracka and order room service. Watch Patriot Games, then bed.

Sunday 6 June: Melbourne

The Shane Warne Wonder Ball was still big news. On Channel Seven's 'Sportsworld', cricket writer Robert Craddock reported that an incredulous Gatting had returned to the England dressing room and asked rhetorically, 'What's that kid bowling out there?'

Despite the headlines created by Warne, many experts still rated Merv as the best performer in the Australian attack. Whereas the wicket was assisting the spinners, there was nothing in it for the quicker types. Merv was undaunted, bowling with pace, fire, aggression and all those other words that the commentators trot out. He also used two important body parts – his heart and his brain.

Indeed, by using his brain, Merv captured a wicket with the last ball of Sunday's play. Bowling to Gatting, who half-expected a bouncer, he uprooted the batsman's middle stump with a searing yorker. The TV in the corner of my bedroom was still on, albeit with the volume turned down low. I was dozing, but sat bolt upright as Bill Lawry, even on low volume, roared madly about the dismissal. Merv later said he was trying to bowl a short one but lost his footing and it came out as a yorker. I think he was being modest.

Monday 7 June: Old Trafford

Have a good win by 179 runs.

Gooch bats well and makes 133 for England. Gets out handling the ball which turns the game around. Until then, it looked like England could hold on for a draw. Warnie bowls well – 49 overs for the innings for four wickets. I also get four. Billy bowls well, but without luck. BJ picks up one. Warnie also takes a great catch to dismiss Caddick.

Stay in dressing rooms for a couple of hours, then back to hotel. Slip around to Pier Six [?! – IC] for a while, then back to hotel. Finish up about 2 am. A big day – and night.

Monday 7 June: Melbourne

An Australian win against England in a Test match is one of the joys of sports spectating. However, my viewing of the Australian bid for victory was put on hold as I went to a friend's 40th birthday party. It was not a long affair, but I was still disappointed to hear the score was 3/190 when I jumped into the car to drive home. Gooch was still there and England seemed to be making a good fist of saving the game.

I dropped into another friend's house on the way home to catch the post-lunch session on TV. We sat there predicting a draw. We lamented the fact that Merv couldn't snare Hick despite working him over in a lion-hearted spell and, as for Gooch, we just couldn't see how he was going to get out. Suddenly, Gooch showed us a way we hadn't considered – he *handled* the ball!

As Merv said in his diary entry, this was the turning point in the match. Merv deservedly picked up Hick shortly after and then came back to finish off the innings by claiming Caddick and Such. As Border scooped up the catch to get rid of Such, I expected to see Merv come thundering down the wicket to embrace the skipper.

Instead, he turned on his heels, sprinted to the stumps and grabbed two souvenirs.

Sticking his tongue in a teammate's ear is an old trick that Merv has dropped from his act. 'I haven't done that for two years,' he said. However, one old trick is still in his repertoire and it was the last thing I saw on the telecast that night. As Shane Warne was picking up his Man of the Match award, Merv could be seen tipping a can of beer over Bobby Simpson.

Australia 289 (M. Taylor 124, M. Slater 58; P. Such 6/67) and 5/432 dec. (I. Healy 102 not out, D. Boon 93, S. Waugh 78 not out, M. Waugh 64) d. England 210 (G. Gooch 65; S. Warne 4/51, M. Hughes 4/59) and 332 (G. Gooch 133; S. Warne 4/86, M. Hughes 4/92) by 179 runs. Man of the Match: Shane Warne.

AFTER the joy of winning the first Test, the Australians rolled on to Birmingham for a three-day match against Warwickshire. In a far-sighted and warmly welcomed piece of programming, the 1993 tour allowed for a day off after each of the six Tests. In 1989, there were occasions when the players had to front up after five days of hard-fought Test cricket and a long night of celebrating.

One story doing the rounds after the '89 tour concerned David Boon and his attempt to take a simple catch at short leg on the morning after one of the Tests. According to the story, Boon was so tired he simply fell over and missed the ball completely. Returning to the pages of Merv's diary, we find there are no such stories this time around.

Dear Merv

I felt I just had to write to you and say how much I enjoyed your performance in the first Test at Old Trafford.

After enduring many hours of watching stereo-type medium pace 'trundlers' in the English game, it was a sheer delight to see some real hostile fast bowling.

I feel very strongly that international cricket should be played with the pride, passion and fire shown by your self in the first Test.

Well done. Best of luck for the rest of the tour.

Yours sincerely
M.E. (Farmer, club player and 'cricket nut')
Gloucestershire

Tuesday 8 June: Birmingham

Start the day with a huge breakfast after watching what I've been eating for the past couple of weeks. Two-hour bus trip to Birmingham. Play cards with Ziggy before watching West Coast Eagles–St Kilda game on video.

Check into Hyatt Hotel. Roomie this game is Ziggy. Although I have the game off, I prefer to stay with the team. Do interview with the Mirror then have room-service lunch. Play golf at Edgbaston golf course with AB, Babsie, Simmo, Ziggy, Unit and Des Rundle. Have a skins game with Unit and Des. Unit ends up with eight, Des five and me four. Great layout, ordinary golf.

Back to hotel for room-service dinner then watch movies with Ziggy until 2 am. The line-up is Switch, New Jack

City and some shocking show called Roots of Evil. [What a way to unwind after the rigours of a Test match! – IC]

Wednesday 9 June: Birmingham

Sleep in until about 10. Have some breakfast and go for a walk. [What a way to unwind after the rigours of a skins game! – IC] End up jumping in a taxi and heading to the cricket. Stay there until just after tea. We bat first and make 4/260-odd.

Drop boots into boot repairer on way back to hotel. Sleep for a couple of hours, get up and go to bar, then out for Indian dinner with Simmo, Maysie and Des. Great place and good food.

Thursday 10 June: Birmingham

Lazy day. Sleep most of day. Only get up to have a shave. Watch boxing and golf on TV. Have some room service and watch a couple of movies on the in-house video channel.

Boys have Warwickshire 8/184 with Maysie taking three wickets.

Friday 11 June: Birmingham

Rain, so no play at all in third day of Warwickshire game. Called off after an early lunch. Leave Birmingham for Bristol where we meet Gloucestershire. Get in about 3 pm and sit around watching TV for a while. Shower up after a shaving cream fight with Unit, my roomie for this game. [Just when I thought that too many cricket traditions were being destroyed, my faith was restored by boys being boys! – IC]

Walk across the road to the College Tavern for a couple of beers, play pool and pinball, then go out for dinner at a seafood place with Junior, BJ and Unit. After dinner, walk around looking for a pub and end up back at the College Tavern.

[As I was due to fly to London in a couple of days, I rang Merv for the last time before departing. He gave me the run-down of the last few days and I remarked that he should be feeling sufficiently rested and rejuvenated after the first Test. 'I suppose so,' he yawned down the phone, 'but a bit more sleep wouldn't go astray.' I asked him if there was anything else to report. 'Oh yeah,' he said matter-of-factly, 'Warnie and Simone just got engaged.' It was all happening for Warne – Man of the Match in the first Test and now a love-match with his blonde girlfriend Simone Callahan. From 20,000 kms away, I detected the faint hum of the tabloid printing presses whirring into motion.– IC]

Australia 7/317 dec. (D. Martyn 116) v.
Warwickshire 8/184 (T. May 3/58). Match drawn.

Saturday 12 June: Bristol

First day of match against Gloucestershire. Overnight rain causes a half-hour delay. We win the toss and bowl. Lose a bit more time because of rain. At the end of the day,

Gloucestershire are 7/190. Warnie takes four wickets, I get two and Maysie one.

Bit of light relief when the team pulls a prank on Billy. Maysie and Tugga buy big slide-on ears and give them to everyone except Billy. While he's walking back to his mark for the last ball of an over, we slip the ears on. He turns and sees us. Everyone cracks up. I guess you had to be there.

Back to hotel, room service with Unit and watch a couple of movies – Doc Hollywood and Hitman. Not bad shows.

Sunday 13 June: Bristol

Second day of Gloucestershire game. We bowl them out for 211. Warnie ends up with five, I get four. Unit and Babsie get us off to a good start and by the end of the day we are 9/400. I get 46 not out at the end. [Including five 4s and two 6s. – IC]

Back to the hotel and watch a western on Sky movie channel. Order room service and watch 'The Addams Family'. [Meanwhile, back in Melbourne, I was boarding Qantas flight QF9 bound for England. Awaiting me was an unexplored world of cricket, video movie viewing and room service. – IC]

Monday 14 June: Bristol

Last day of Gloucestershire game. Overnight rain and constant rain throughout the day results in no play at all. [Two consecutive wash-outs were a setback to Australia's bid to grab the $100,000 bonus on offer for winning 10 of the 14 three-day county matches. – IC]

Bright spot of the day is provided by the 'Hey! Hey! It's Saturday' crew. Molly Meldrum, Trevor Marmalade and Plucka Duck turn up at the ground to film a few segments. Plucka joins in fielding and catching practice. When play is delayed, Billy, Warnie and myself go out and bowl to Plucka. Very entertaining stuff. [Strangely, Merv made no mention of the fact that Plucka was in all sorts of trouble against McDermott and Warne, but he managed to hit the ball straight back past Merv with consummate ease. Not a problem. – IC]

After lunch, hop on the bus and head for London. Another 48 Hours and Terminator 2 are featured on the video. Get into the hotel in mid-afternoon and have a sleep. Rooming with Heals this time around. Out to an Italian place for dinner with Heals, BJ and Billy. The river in this city looks even dirtier than the Yarra.

Tuesday 15 June: London

Leave the hotel at 9 am and head to Lord's for practice. Walking across the ground to get to the nets, find that the ground is soaked. Do warm-up, then train for two and a half hours. [For Merv, it was a different story to seven weeks ago when the Australian team arrived for the first training session at Lord's and he was unable to bowl. Now he was right back in the action. – IC] Bowl off short run-up because of wet ground.

After training, boys get done up in suits to go to the National Sporting Club luncheon at Cafe Royal. Sign about three million autographs. Not a bad day. Back to hotel, then go out for a haircut. Come back, watch TV, then jump in a taxi and go to a pub for a meal and a few drinks with Heals, BJ and Junior. AB, Tubby and Unit also there. Catch taxi home. Stop for a Mac Attack on the way.

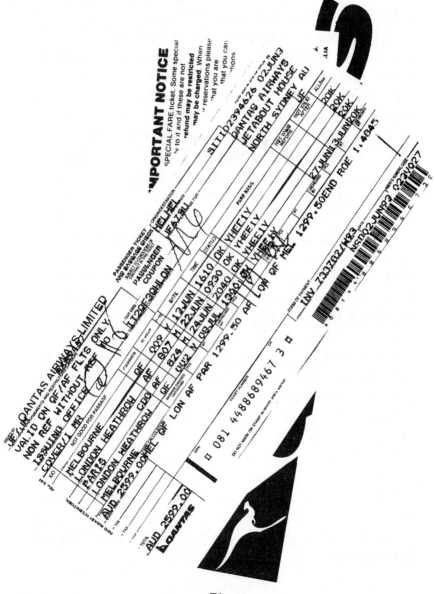

[Having arrived in London and recovered from the jet lag, I rang Merv that morning. I was too late – the team had left for the nets at Lord's. I took the opportunity to do a spot of sight-seeing and headed for the city on a double-decker bus. I did all the tourist things: Picadilly Circus, Trafalgar Square, the Tower of London, St Paul's Cathedral, Big Ben, the House of Commons.

Walking past the entrance to the car park at the House of Commons, I noticed a crowd including several TV crews. One of the cameramen told me they were expecting the Prime Minister, John Major, to arrive at any minute. I stopped and waited. I knew who I was looking for – the PM's photo was in the morning papers almost as many times as Merv's! That seemed to suggest the cricket was big news, but, oddly enough, when I grabbed an afternoon paper to read on the bus on the way home, I couldn't find a word in it anywhere about the Lord's Test starting in two days. When I arrived home, I rang Merv at the team hotel and he told me about the National Sporting Club luncheon. The guest speaker had been the sports editor of the same paper I'd read on the bus. Merv was not a big wrap for him: 'I'm not surprised his paper's got no cricket in it,' Merv said.

The subject switched to the book and, enthused by my sight-seeing, I suggested to Merv that we could get some great photos of him at famous London landmarks. 'What about after nets tomorrow? It'll only take an hour or so,' I said. Merv was less enthusiastic. 'Sorry, mate,' he said, 'I'd love to, but I get too nervous before a Test. I also like to rest up and get as much sleep as possible. I do the same before Shield games, too.' Resting was fair enough, but I was surprised by Merv's confession about nerves. However, it just goes to show that nerves afflict big fast bowlers, even after 45 Tests. – IC]

Wednesday 16 June: London

Heavy overnight rain puts 9 am training on hold until 2 pm. Sleep. More rain throughout the day and training is cancelled. More sleep. Get up for team meeting at 6 pm. Team meetings are conducted in an informal sort of way with everyone in attendance – not just the Test XII. AB and Simmo sit out the front and the rest of us make contributions from around the room. They usually start by running through the opposition line-up, discussing the strengths and weaknesses of their batsmen. We talk about how to get them out, how we've got them out before and different fielding positions for different players. For example, Heals suggests, 'Bowl spin to Robin Smith.' [It must have been a race to see who could come up with that one first. As for Merv, did he offer any specific ideas? 'Oh, yeah. I thought Hick might be vulnerable to the short ball and I mentioned that a couple of times.' – IC]

All the England players are known to us from past tours or county experience. Junior is particularly helpful with his observations of blokes he has encountered while playing for Essex. The information is good for new players such as Slats and BJ coming into the team as well as reinforcing things in the senior players' minds.

Out for team dinner at an American sort of place. Spare ribs, barbecue chicken, chicken wings, that sort of stuff. Back to hotel, watch TV.

While Merv calmed his nerves by sleeping, I was getting uptight about the rain. I'd flown halfway around the world to fulfill a long-time ambition of seeing Australia and England locked in cricketing combat at Lord's and the rain was threatening to wash it all away. Clearly, sleep was not going to work for me. Instead, I went shopping.

The last message from Merv before I headed to

Harrod's was that training would start at 2 pm. If it was wet, he said, training would move to the indoor nets. A few hours later, I emerged from St John's Wood station, the nearest stop to Lord's, and walked into a deluge. Fair dinkum, it was bucketing down. Even if it stopped then, I thought, they would be lucky to play the next day. Amid the frustration and despair, I still felt excited about being so near the famous ground so I hailed a taxi and told the driver to take me there. Cricket players and watchers who have made the pilgrimage to Lord's from all parts of the world must have their own special memory of the first time they walked through the Grace Gates. Mine is huddling under an umbrella and telling a bloke I was looking for the Australian cricket team. To which he replied, 'You won't find 'em here. They cancelled training.'

'What about the indoor nets, then?' I asked.

'No, they couldn't get in. We're setting up corporate hospitality suites in there,' he said.

The excitement of a few minutes earlier had disappeared somewhat. I splashed my way back to St John's Wood station and went home to ring Merv. 'That's a bit of bad luck,' he said when I related my rain-soaked saga. 'You would have enjoyed seeing the boys in the nets.'

'There's one thing I would have enjoyed more than that,' I said, 'and that would have been seeing one of them with a spare ticket for tomorrow.' At the other end of the line, Merv let out a huge sigh as his mind flashed back to the farewell dinner. The ticket crunch had arrived and, as he predicted, I'd come to him in my hour of need. There was a long pause, then Merv uttered those three words I'd been hoping for: 'Not a problem.'

Mr Merv Hughes
Australian Test Team
c/- Vistor's Dressing Room
Lord's Cricket Ground
London

Dear Mr Hughes
   Congratulations to you and the rest of the team on your recent Test victory. Your bowling performance was again splendidly effective and your dismissal of Mike Gatting, last ball of the day, was especially appreciated by those of us who think that he is an old fart (but not too old to go to India ... nuff said.) As soon as Gooch and Gatting crossed mid-wicket, I said to my boyfriend, 'I bet Hughes clean bowls him.' And lo and behold, you duly obliged.
   May I add that despite the fierce image your mass of facial hair presents, I have noticed that you have the most beautiful, gentle come-to-bed eyes that I have seen for a long time. (I bet all the girls say that!)
   Thank you for taking the time to read my daft prattlings. All the best to you and your team mates.

Yours sincerely

J.F. (Miss)
Edinburgh

PS. I do love English cricket really.

Dear Mr Hughes

I write as an England fan but I have to admit your dismissal of Mike Gatting with the last ball of Sunday's play was a super piece of cricket.

After the incidents of the previous few minutes, he, and I, and thousands of others were expecting that ball to be up round his ears, it wasn't!

Although it may have cost us the game, I enjoyed that moment, as a cricket fan. Well done.

Yours sincerely

RD
Cambridge

4 Living It Up At Lord's

EVERYTHING was right with the world – I was going to Lord's, the rain had stopped, play would start on time and Merv had kindly offered to leave a ticket at the gate for me.

The train to St John's Wood was packed with cricket-goers. Men in jackets with the distinctive orange and yellow MCC ties were scattered around the carriage. They had to be England supporters although I'm sure if you asked them whether they wanted the home side to win, they would have replied, 'I don't mind who wins as long as it's a good game.' The Aussie supporters also were prominent, their shorts and T-shirts a dead giveaway.

Deciding I needed a newspaper to finish off my preparation, I picked up a copy of the *Daily Mirror*, mainly because of the front page blurb which said: 'Merv Hughes writes for us'. On page 36, the headline proclaimed: I'LL LORD IT OVER POMS. Underneath this, a sub-heading declared: 'Sumo to take grip on England'. In the article, Merv described how the 'Sumo' nickname had been coined by the crowd at Old Trafford during the first Test and that it had even caught on among his teammates.

Merv wrote: 'I suppose I've always had a love–hate relationship with crowds all over the world. I love them –

and they hate me! But it's good knock-about stuff and, in any case, I like to build up a rapport with the fans.

'The last time I was here on our '89 Ashes tour it seemed that the atmosphere was a little bit too down-beat for my liking. Not now. The atmosphere at Old Trafford in the first Test plus the one-dayers quickly changed all that and now I expect Lord's to be the same.

'I don't know what the members will think of the 'Sumo' chants ringing around the famous old ground, but that's nothing compared to some other fans. They've been chanting at me: "You fat bastard, you fat bastard, you ate all our pies!" Maybe it's the way I look at 6ft 3in and weighing in at just over 17 stone.

'I get some stick wherever I go in the game, but the fans pay their money and are entitled to their opinions. In any case, I'm happy just as long as it doesn't go over the top, although there are plenty of Aussie fans around to set the record straight.

'Maybe it's also the way I play my cricket with a will to win like all Aussies. And then maybe it's the way I go about the business that gets them going.

'Some people think I sent Graeme Hick on his way with a mouthful at Old Trafford, but really I let rip with my appeal until I was virtually eye-balling him. It was a crucial wicket – at a crucial stage – and a great one for me so I reacted in a way that, on reflection, might have looked bad on the television replay. Maybe it was, but it happens at times in different sports when the pressure is at its fiercest.

'I'm no different, but my teammates wouldn't have it any other way and that's all that matters.'

As the train pulled in to St John's Wood station, I was pumped up for action. So was Merv, judging by the content and tone of his column in the *Mirror*! As events turned out, however, the Australian batsmen didn't allow him a chance to do anything for a couple of days. We return to Merv's diary for the five days of the Lord's Test along with my daily impressions, this time from the scene of the action.

Thursday 17 June: Lord's

Off to Lord's for the first day of the second Test – and what a day it is. We win the toss and bat with Slats and Tubby getting off to a great start. Their stand is worth 260. Slats gets 152 and Tubby 111. At stumps, we're 2/292 with Junior and Babsie at the wicket.

Sit around for most of the day watching the openers in

action. Cove calls me down to the pavilion door for a chat during the morning. Good to see him, but not as good as seeing Sue. She arrives and comes straight to the ground. Catch up with her after play in the Lord's Tavern. Warnie and Simone there too. Go out for dinner with them, then back to hotel.

Thursday 17 June: Lord's

Merv didn't let me down. My ticket was waiting in an envelope at a window in the wall over which hung a sign saying 'Ticket Collection Point'. It was no ordinary envelope. Made of thick brown paper, the front was printed with old English letters and the MCC logo. This was a souvenir in itself, a tangible piece of Lord's tradition.

My seat was on the upper deck of the Compton Stand which is at the opposite end to the Members' pavilion – and the ticket collection window. This meant walking back in the direction from which I'd just come. Fortunately, walking around the outside of Lord's is equivalent to about half the distance around the MCG.

I entered through a gate near the Nursery, which some people mistakenly believe refers to the practice wickets being there to provide a nursery for young cricketers. The real story is that the site upon which Lord's is situated was a market garden when Thomas Lord bought the land last century, and a nursery for young plants could be found where the practice wickets are today.

Having dispensed with that bit of cricket trivia, I

headed for my seat. It turned out to be in the midst of a group of Australians, several of whom were instantly recognisable. Next to me, for example, was former Test spinner Ray Bright, who was chatting to current player Paul Reiffel, while over my left shoulder was Victorian wicket-keeper Darren Berry. It was a cosy little Victorian enclave.

Out in the middle, a couple of New South Welshman – or, more specifically, Wagga-ites – Mark Taylor and Michael Slater opened up in bright fashion. By lunch, they had taken Australia's score to 0/100 and there was a feeling we were about to witness something special.

The break provided the chance for a stroll to the champagne bar at the Nursery end where the atmosphere was akin to Oaks Day during the Melbourne Cup carnival. A rough conversion showed the prices of the bubbly refreshments to be: $50 a bottle, $30 a half-bottle, and $10 a glass. The area was peopled predominantly by dashing young men in navy blue suits holding a glass of champers in one hand and a mobile telephone in the other. 'We're having lunch at Lord's,' one fellow bellowed into his phone as if he was speaking from a trendy restaurant, rather than the famous cricket ground.

There were more sights to behold. At the other end, behind the old pavilion, scores of members were partaking of picnic lunches on a manicured patch of ground not unlike a croquet lawn. There was a lovely touch about this as the members placed their wicker baskets, cooler boxes (the English term for Esky) and woollen rugs on the lawn when they arrived in the morning. They then went off to watch the play knowing that the sandwiches were safe under the watchful eye of an MCC steward.

After lunch, Taylor and Slater kept the runs flowing at such a rate that Slater reached his 100 by the middle of the session. It was, in fact, 10 minutes before three o'clock or 10 to midnight (AEST) when he posted the magical three figures. We've all heard of players making a century before lunch, but here was a new claim to fame – a ton before midnight at home.

As the crowd stood to acknowledge Slater's performance, a young man in front of me was applauding as generously as anyone. He was Matthew Hayden, the rookie opener beaten for a berth by Slater. A couple of rows back, a dark-haired young woman also was cheering and clapping wildly. Earlier, I had noticed her gazing intently at the centre wicket action. Even at the end of an over, her attention could not be diverted from the players or, to be accurate, one player in particular. Later, I found out she was Michael Slater's fiancée, Stephanie.

England did not look like getting a wicket, but the home supporters retained their sense of humour. At 3.15, with the score on 0/192, an announcement came over the public address calling for Matthew Church of the MCC staff to report to the secretary's office. From up the back of the stand, an English voice demanded: 'Bring him on, bring him on!' Five minutes later, Taylor smacked Phil Tufnell for consecutive boundaries to bring up the Australian 200. This was the signal for another English voice to cry out in mock despair, 'That's it, they can declare now. We can't possibly get that many.'

Play rolled on, the runs kept coming and the scoreboard provided a rare sight: Australia 0/258, MA Taylor 100, MJ Slater 150. Cameras clicked around the ground to capture the evidence. Perhaps the cameras distracted Slater for he was caught a few moments later after scoring a magnificent innings of 152. The opening stand of 260 was a record for Australia at Lord's. I'd have been happy to travel halfway around the world just for this day; the great thing was I had four more to savour.

About five minutes before stumps, there was another example of what makes Lord's so different from cricket in Australia when the last announcement for the day came over the PA. This time patrons were asked 'to assist the ground staff by placing litter in the bins provided on the way out'. Such a request at the MCG or SCG would be greeted by all manner of rubbish being hurled into the air. At Lord's, though, I picked up my steak and kidney pie wrapper – not to mention feeling compelled to collect the plastic beer cups, soft drink cans and ice cream wrappers dropped by people who had left early!

Friday 18 June: Lord's

Leave for ground at 9 am. Do warm-up, then sit on bum for rest of the day. Junior gets out bowled by Tufnell for 99. Border makes 77, getting out to something that resembles a golf shot more than cricket. Boon gets 130-odd not out. By the end of play, we're 4/590-odd.

Lowlight, though, when Billy goes to hospital with bad stomach cramps. Exploratory surgery removes a piece of twisted intestine. Really bad news.

After play, meet Sue and Simone in Lord's Tavern. Have a drink there, then out to an Italian restaurant. Taxi back to hotel with Warnie about 11.30.

[Several players were accompanied on various stages of the tour by their wives, fiancées or girlfriends. Actually, 'accompanied' is probably not quite the right word because the ACB disapproves of the women staying at the same hotel as the players. It's an attitude that provokes much debate, but we're not about to get involved in an argument here. Please direct your correspondence to the ACB. – IC]

MARYLEBONE CRICKET CLUB
Lord's Cricket Ground, London, NW8 8QN.

This envelope is for collection at the Ticket Collection Point

DATE	17/6/93	MATCH	2ND TEST

NAME	IAN COVER
ORGANISATION (If applicable)	
REFERENCE	1 TICKET
THIS ENVELOPE WAS DEPOSITED BY	M. HUGHES

If uncollected, this envelope should be returned to the M.C.C. Club Office.

Friday 18 June: Lord's

On the second day, I made my entrance through the Grace Gates and walked around to the Compton Stand via the Members' pavilion. The previous day, I'd spotted plenty of familiar faces from Australia and this morning was no exception. As soon as I came through the gate I saw Richie Benaud heading my way, a vision in pastel. In a sea of navy suits and dark blazers, it was impossible to miss him decked out splendidly in his trademark white jacket teamed with a pinkish-mauve shirt and pale blue slacks. In my head, I heard myself saying, 'Good outfit, that.'

The star-spotting didn't finish there. Later in the day, an Australian acquaintance pointed out that two-fifths of the Rolling Stones were sitting in a private box on the other side of the ground. Sure enough, there were Mick Jagger and Charlie Watts flanking Imran Khan and watching the Australian score grind on towards 600.

As day two drew to a close, the England fans were battling to display any reserves of good humour. However, late in the afternoon, one supporter managed to brighten up proceedings with the following observation: 'Well played, chaps! You got two wickets yesterday, two today and you might get two more tomorrow – at that rate, you'll have them all out by the end of the week!'

After play, I was drawn again to the Lord's Tavern where the bar-room experts were debating whether Australia had batted for too long. A popular line of argument was that Border should have declared at tea and given his bowlers a crack at the England top order. A man, overhearing my circle of friends discussing the issue, elbowed his way in and said, 'They couldn't declare – McDermott's crook.'

During the next half-hour, the discussions in the bar switched from the subject of the declaration to the state of McDermott's health. Depending on who you talked to, the fast bowler was suffering from a recurrence of a groin problem, a burst appendix, a perforated ulcer, a twisted bowel, a ruptured hernia or plain old food poisoning. Speculation gave way to facts when Merv arrived in the bar and confirmed that McDermott had gone to hospital for exploratory surgery. It was not good news and quelled the revelry among those who were celebrating Australia's batting exploits.

Later, I heard that McDermott had been in pain for several days. On the Tuesday night, he had been doubled over and writhing in agony on his hotel room floor. His roommate Paul Reiffel, who had seen Merv suffering from pre-match nerves, initially thought McDermott was suffering from the same condition – only a lot worse. After a while, though, he realised something was seriously wrong.

Saturday 19 June: Lord's

Another good day for us as we declare at 4/632 with Boon getting a big hundred and Tugga 20 not out. By the end of the day, England are 9/190 with everyone bowling well. Warnie takes four wickets, I get three and Maysie two. It's also a great fielding day for us with Maysie taking a great catch to get Gooch. Robin Smith becomes the first player to be given out by the third umpire in a Test in England – stumped off May.

With Billy out, Junior is my partner with the new ball. I think he chokes a bit with a number of no-balls early on!

Meet Sue and Simone in Lord's Tavern after play then go to visit Billy in hospital. Maysie and Heals are there when we arrive. Nice hospital and he's in good hands. Leave the hospital and head off to the place where Sue is staying. Order dial-a-pizza and it's a good quality one. Catch taxi back to the Westbury about 11.

Saturday 19 June: Lord's

Every new day in a Test brings with it the prospect of unknown wonders. And as I took up my accustomed position in the Compton Stand on day three at Lord's, I

Ziggy Zoehrer and Molly Meldrum in the rooms at Lord's.

Rolling Stones drummer Charlie Watts, BJ and Simmo at Lord's. BJ's too young to remember the Stones, but Simmo's an old rocker.

Slats and Tubby look pretty relaxed before they go back out after lunch on the first day of the second Test at Lord's.

A bit of Aussie ingenuity records three new hundreds.

Maysie hops into a hot dog at Wimbledon. Sorry, the dietician wasn't supposed to see this one.

Me and my beautiful wife Sue at Wimbledon.

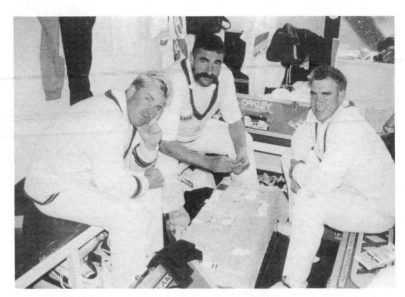

Playing Monopoly with Warnie and Unit at Hampshire.

'Ebony and ivory, go together in bowling harmony.' Third Test, Trent Bridge.

Cracka Holdsworth with his hat-trick ball at Derby.

The girls do a bit of celebrating after the fourth Test at Headingley.

Easy money. The journos on tour who lost £136 in various bets with me at Neath.

Me and Plucka. Managed to avoid him until the second last match of the tour against Essex.

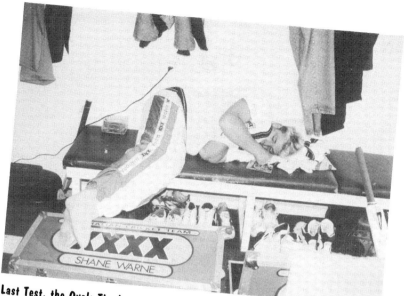

Last Test, the Oval: Tiredness sets in. Warnie is worn out after bowling 400 overs. He dreams about going home.

One for the record — the bowlers line up at the Oval: (from left) Cracka, Warnie, BJ, me, Maysie and Pistol.

Warnie receives Man of the Series award at the Oval.

This is what it's all about. The boys with replicas of the Ashes presented at the end of the tour.

couldn't help thinking we were going to see more than our share of cricketing delights. Of the most interest was seeing how Merv would handle the challenge and responsibility of carrying the pace attack on his own. And would Shane Warne cast his spinning spell over the England batsmen again? Or was the pitch, so obviously full of runs, also going to produce a 600-plus total for England, thus reducing the match to a draw?

The question about Merv's role as the solo spearhead of the attack was answered quickly. The big fellow, putting plenty of grunt into his bowling, dug one in short and Gooch couldn't resist the temptation to hook. The ball flew to fine leg where Tim May grabbed the chance with both hands after covering a lot of ground. The catch itself was memorable, but even more indelibly etched in my mind was the sight of his 10 teammates, headed by Merv, running in a V formation to embrace him. It was a magic moment.

At lunch, I met a few friends from Australia who, like me, were fulfilling an ambition to see a Lord's Test. We were enjoying a drink in the Father Time Bar when someone noticed the players were back on the field. My word, the 40 minutes at lunch had whizzed past! On the first two days, you could stay in the bar for as long as you liked. All you were missing was Australia making run after run after run. However, with England batting and May extracting turn, you were bound to miss something if you lingered at the bar for 'just one more quick pint'.

Sure enough, something did happen. May spun one past Gatting's bat and the former England captain was bowled for the third time in three innings in the series. And he fell to his third conqueror, Warne and Hughes having done the damage in the first Test. Fortunately, there was a TV in the bar and, much to our joy, we saw the action replayed several times. It was time, though, to return to my seat for the 'live' action.

Border decided to go for spin at both ends and Warne was introduced. This not only added to England's batting woes, but also produced a marvellous verbal exchange in the crowd. Channel Nine may have its Classic Catches competition, but this was straight out of Classic Quips. In the middle of an over from Warne, an English voice to my left taunted the leg spinner thus: 'You're bowling rubbish, Warne!' To which a distinctly female, definitely Australian voice up the back retorted, 'Get stuffed!' When Warne's fiancé Simone rolled up and sat in front of me, I told her the story. She laughed and said, 'Yeah, I know. It was me!'

I must admit that I didn't see the entire day's play. I'd made arrangements to meet some friends at another sporting event and slipped away at three o'clock. Mind you, with the score at 3/107, I felt we were in a pretty strong position and the boys could look after themselves.

The other sporting event I attended was a match between the London Hawks and the Earl's Court Roos in the British Australian Rules Football League. The Hawks proved too good in the match played in a park near the Royal Botanic Gardens in Kew. Cricket was being played in the area, too, and we saw the Kew Cricket Club in action as we walked away from the football. A sign on the clubhouse wall said 'Kew CC circa 1737'. That's 50 years before the First Fleet arrived at Botany Bay. What history! What tradition!

About half a dozen old-timers were sitting on deck-chairs in front of the Kew clubhouse. The area around their chairs was bordered by a low picket fence which carried a sign saying 'Members only'. Making sure I stayed outside the designated area, I inquired of a gentlemen with a transistor if he knew the score at Lord's. 'Yes, my boy,' he said, 'it's 9/189.' I asked him who had taken the wickets. With an air of resignation, the gentleman uttered a one-word reply: 'Warne.'

Sunday 20 June: Lord's

Have an OK day. Pick up last wicket of innings after 25 minutes of play. England follow on and bat well with Gooch and Atherton getting them off to another good start. Warnie gets the breakthrough – Gooch, caught behind. Atherton is run out for 99. [Courtesy of big Merv's big throw from the deep. – IC] Smith goes to a good catch at bat-pad by Unit, who is subbing for McDermott.

England ends the day at 3/230 with Gatting and Hick at the crease. A day in the field with no luck. Things will have to go better for us tomorrow. Ice up knee and jump in bath.

Drop in to see Sue at Lord's Tavern, then jump on bus back to hotel. AB, Marto, BJ and a few others get off at hospital to see Billy. Get back to hotel, order room service. A quiet night.

Sunday 20 June: Lord's

If Merv had a quiet night, then I had a quiet morning. All this cricket watching must have been catching up with me. For a change of pace, I accepted a friend's invitation to check out a local market on the way to Lord's. The market was an amazing affair. Situated in Camden, there were shops and stalls crammed into a couple of blocks on either side of a filthy canal. The main street through the shopping centre was over-run by people spilling out on to the roadway, forcing cars to crawl along at a snail's pace.

Most of the stall holders seemed to have a ghettoblaster playing very loud music. If the idea was to attract customers, I'm sorry to report that they simply drove me away. Only one stall managed to hold my interest for more than a minute thanks to the man in charge having his radio tuned to the BBC's cricket coverage. Mind you, the news wasn't very exciting. England was 1/171 and giving every indication that they could force a draw.

Eventually, we tore ourselves away from the marvels of the market and marched off to Lord's. We arrived after tea and headed for the gate behind the Nursery, but were surprised to find about 50 or so men queuing to gain entry. At that stage of the day, I thought we would simply roll up and stroll in. My friend decided to find out what was going on, so he called one of the men aside and said, 'What's the queue for, mate?' The man asked him to repeat the question, so he did. The man, having twigged that my friend was Australian, spat out the answer: 'We go in the gate, they give us a brush in one hand, a shovel in the other and we clean up your shit!' We had, in our colonial ignorance, stumbled across the queue for those less fortunate inhabitants of London who wish to help clean up the ground after play. We didn't hang around to discuss minimum pay rates, but the impression given by these gents indicated it wasn't in the top range.

The next gate was the one we wanted and we walked in without further incident. Alas, we had missed the run-out of Atherton as Gatting and Hick were at the wicket. A man in the crowd filled us in on the details of Merv's marvellous throw from the outfield which resulted in Atherton's demise just one run short of his century. Later, outside the Lord's Tavern, I bumped into Ian

Healy and asked him about the dramatic dismissal. Interestingly, he revealed that he was unaware of any drama. 'The ball gets thrown in to me hundreds of times a day and I treat them all the same,' Healy said. 'Sure, there was a bit of yelling going on, but I had to concentrate on taking the ball cleanly and then breaking the stumps. The moment you worry about where the batsman is or you start getting excited, you're gone.' Mind you, he did admit to being excited after Atherton was given out. 'We all were,' he said.

I must make an admission myself and that is that a couple of pints had turned me in to an expert and I was keen to share my new-found expertise with Healy. 'Well, I've got it all worked out for tomorrow,' I told him. 'Two wickets in the first session, two in the second and three in the last.' Healy thought about it for a moment, then put me in my place. 'What's wrong with two in the first and five in the second?' he said. A good point, I thought, emphasising why he's playing for Australia and I'm spectating.

Healy excused himself to board the team bus. A minute or so later, Merv, struck by the realisation that the bus was leaving, emerged from the bar. The race was on. Would Merv make it to the bus before it pulled away from the kerb? Cheered on by a happy throng of Australian supporters in front of the pub, the big fellow hit the footpath running. It was going to be close. Merv drew level with the back of the bus just as it started moving. The players thought it was a great joke and I'll bet they were telling the driver to keep going. Twenty metres, 30 metres . . . then, hooray, it lurched to a stop. Merv let out a huge sigh of relief as the door swung open. He reached the steps, turned, waved and, to the roar of the pub crowd, disappeared inside.

Monday 21 June: Lord's

We can go 2–0 up in the series by taking seven wickets today. Everyone knows how important it is to get Gatting early. Warnie does this by trapping him in front for 70-odd. Hick and Stewart get 60 each. Stewart and Foster hang around for a while after lunch. There's two things you can do – keep plugging away or try something different. In this case, we try something different and AB gives himself a bowl. It works.

We win just before tea with Warnie and Maysie getting four wickets. AB gets one and there's a run out. Put on the blazers to meet the Queen on the ground in front of the pavilion followed by the presentations. Slats is Man of the Match for his 150 on the first day. A big thrill for him.

Go inside for a couple of hours to celebrate. Meet Sue at the Lord's Tavern later and head out for an Italian feed with her, Simone and Warnie. After dinner, the team goes out to the Windmill for a few beers. [Just a few? – IC] Back to hotel after midnight. [Well after midnight! – IC]

Monday 21 June: Lord's

My expert opinion – so readily offered to Ian Healy – that Australia would take the seven wickets needed for victory sounded good last night. However, in the cold light of the morning, I couldn't help feeling that England might just hang on for the day and force a draw. Given England's woeful record in recent Tests, this would be a cause for celebration among English supporters. Thus, it was surprising to find the ground was so empty when we arrived for the last day. You could only conclude that the fans expected to lose. And you couldn't help thinking that this defeatist attitude had pervaded the England players.

Anyway, that was their worry. I was at Lord's to enjoy myself. With such a small crowd in attendance, it was easy to move around and I had a perfect opportunity to get right down to the fence at fine leg where Merv was fielding. Perfect for photos for the book. In a bizarre twist, the MCC had stationed a steward in the exact spot where I wanted to go. Can you believe it? On a day when the crowd consisted of the proverbial three men and a dog, there was a steward stopping people going in to a public section! 'But I only want to take a couple of photos,' I protested. No go. By a stroke of good luck, this public section abutted the Members' and a chap, who had overheard my plight, invited me to come over to his side. 'Jolly decent of you, sir,' I said.

His name was Alan and he was sitting in the front row with two friends, Patrick and Tony. They asked me if I knew Merv and I said I did. 'Well, do you think you could get him to give us a smile then?' asked Alan. 'We've been sitting here for five days and he hasn't smiled once.' 'Not a problem,' I said. At this stage, Merv was about 10 metres in from the fence directly in front of us so I called out, 'Hey, Merv, give these blokes a smile, will ya?' He finished walking in with the bowler, turned and strode towards us with a scowl. I could tell my English friends were unimpressed with my claim about knowing Merv. Just as I was ready to let fly with a sarcastic 'thanks mate', a huge grin broke out across Merv's dial and the Englishmen were delighted.

For the next three or four overs, my wife clicked

away merrily whenever Merv was at fine leg. I perched myself on the fence so I'd be in the foreground of the photos while, in the background, Merv smiled, waved and pulled faces for the camera. Alan, Patrick and Tony were highly amused to be treated to a private performance by Merv. Patrick even allowed me to don his MCC blazer for one of the photos, an act which I feared might lead to his membership being rescinded.

After half an hour of these hi-jinx, I started to also fear that we were distracting Merv from the task at hand – bowling out the Poms. So, I adjourned to the Compton Stand to watch the last few overs before lunch and wickets fell immediately. Hick went followed by Lewis, who jumped down the track to May, changed his mind and tried to defend. He missed and Healy did the rest. Lewis trudged off without bothering the scorers in either innings of the match.

I went for a walk during the lunch break in the hope that I might spot someone famous again in the crowd. I was not disappointed. Within 50 metres of leaving the Compton Stand, I recognised a tall man wandering in my direction. He appeared to have just arrived at the ground because he was studying his ticket, trying to work out where to find his seat. He had a puzzled look on his face, a look which I'd seen dozens of times in sketches on 'Monty Python's Flying Circus' and in episodes of 'Fawlty Towers'. Yes, it was John Cleese. Curiosity got the better of me and I stopped to watch him climb some stairs. Alas, there was no silly walk.

After lunch, the quest for the remaining four England wickets resumed. A resolute partnership between Stewart and Foster held the Aussies at bay for 75 minutes, but once Border removed Foster, the floodgates opened. Shane Warne wrapped up the Test by bowling both Such and Tufnell around their legs with almost identical deliveries. Marvellous stuff, that! Not only had I come to Lord's to see Australia play a Test match, I'd also seen Australia win.

To complete the total Lord's experience, I was eager to set foot on the hallowed turf and I got the chance when the crowd was invited to come on to the ground for the presentations. A group of us, including Merv's manager David Emerson, climbed the fence and walked towards the pavilion where the players would line up to meet the Queen. As for the surface of the ground, I can tell you it's as magnificent as it looks on television. Smooth, firm and fast, it's more like an enormous putting green than a cricket ground.

By the time we reached the presentation area, the crowd was about 10-deep and it was impossible to see what was happening. However, it soon became clear that the Queen had reached Merv in the line-up as an Australian voice called out, 'Hey Merv! Slip your tongue into that!' For once, I reckon Her Majesty was amused.

The sponsor's cheques were handed out, including the Man of the Match award for Michael Slater, and the players went inside for some private celebrations. The happy fans gathered below the Australian dressing room were not content and they demanded that their heroes appear triumphantly on the balcony. A chant went up: 'Aussie, Aussie, Aussie! Oi, oi, oi!' The players, like true show-business professionals, waited for the curtain calls to reach fever pitch before they came forward to take their bows. The ovation grew loudest when Merv appeared. As an encore, he leaned over the balcony and held up a T-shirt emblazoned with the word 'Sumo'. It was yet another magic moment.

The crowd moved off to raise a victory toast at the nearby Lord's Tavern. When Merv and Shane Warne arrived to join the festivities, they were greeted with more cheers. While the Australians were celebrating en masse, the England players slipped away in their private cars. Unfortunately for them, it was not a quiet, anonymous exit because they had to drive out the gate beside the Lord's Tavern. As a result, they found themselves on the end of some good-natured heckling from the happy horde outside the pub. To their credit, most players gave a cheerful wave before being swallowed up by the traffic flow.

That night, I dined on fish and chips while making some notes about the fantastic five days I had experienced at Lord's. Glancing through my jottings, I noticed that the fish and chips followed nights of pizza, hamburgers and Mexican. I was falling victim to the Merv Hughes Diet!

Australia 4/632 dec. (D. Boon 164 not out, M. Slater 152, M. Taylor 111, M. Waugh 99, A. Border 77) d. England 205 (M. Atherton 80; M. Hughes 4/52, S. Warne 4/57) and 365 (M. Atherton 99; T. May 4/81, S. Warne 4/102) by an innings and 62 runs. Man of the Match: M. Slater.

Dear King Kong

    A few lines to protest at your unsporting bowling actions at Lord's.

    If you think intimidatory style bowling is the correct route to winning games, you should think again.

    But your attitude is typical and won't be tolerated here, rest assured of that.

    Footballers are bringing that game into disrepute by unsporting format and cricket doesn't need to follow suit. Just tell that wicketkeeper pal of yours if his hands are so cold, that he has to keep clapping them, he should go sick.

    Before closing, advise your grumpy captain to endeavour to display a smile on his face some of the time. Like Gouchie [sic.], it's clearly time he took early retirement.

You too, Whisker Bill!
Bye for now

Irate, OAP
Doncaster

5 I'll Take the High Road . . .

THE Lord's Test was over and Merv and I went our separate ways. As the old Scottish song says, I took the high road while Merv and the Australians headed in the opposite direction for a county game at Southampton after brief sojourns at Wimbledon and Oxford.

Tuesday 22 June: Wimbledon Tennis Championship

Sleep in. Get up about 10.30 and pack bags. Bus leaves for Wimbledon at midday. Get there about one o'clock and sit in the players' lounge for a while watching a Jennifer Capriati game. Grab some centre court tickets for Boris Becker versus Marc Goellner. Watch the first two sets then go back up to players' bar. End up in corner bar with BJ, Babs, Heals, Maysie, Marto and Cracka. Great to just sit there and enjoy the view.

Leave Wimbledon about 6.30 pm bound for Oxford. We start a three-day match against Combined Universities tomorrow. Get in about 8.30, rooming with Junior. Watch TV then sleep. [Tennis takes it out of you! – IC]

Wednesday 23 June: Oxford

First day of Combined Uni match. I'm 12th man for the game and quite happy to have a rest. Signing autographs gets a bit hectic, though. Did about a million today. We win toss and bat. Slats follows up his Lord's ton with another one. Marto also gets 100 and Unit 98.

Back to hotel for a shower then out to a hotel appearance. Maysie, Pistol, Warnie and myself do this one. It's a good night at the Baker and Brew House. Catch up with Sue and go out for coffee with her after the pub show.

Thursday 24 June: Oxford

Second day of Combined Uni game. They declare at 7/280-odd and we bat again. Sit around signing autographs for most of the day. Do another million. Emo [Merv's manager David Emerson] drops in with his wife Mary and their son Christopher. Chat about business matters with Emo, then do a photo shoot for the Mirror. [For this assignment, Merv dressed up in leather gear like Arnie Schwarzenegger in The Terminator. That's not all. The look was completed with props as Merv straddled a high-powered motorbike and brandished an equally high-powered machine-gun. When the picture was published, Merv described it as 'a classic'. – IC]

Back to hotel for a shower, then go for a walk around Oxford with Sue. Don't get much chance to look around or soak up local atmosphere while on tour, so make the most of it here. Oxford is a great little town. Finish up at an Italian restaurant for dinner. Not bad. Walk to bed-and-breakfast place where Sue is staying, then get a lift back to team hotel with Slats.

Friday 25 June: Oxford

Last day of Combined Uni game. We bat on to 6/233 declared. Warnie gets among the runs with 47. He's caught on the square leg boundary trying to get his 50 with one over the top. Set them about 330 to win, but we knock them over for less than 200 with a session to spare.

Jump on bus for trip to Southampton for the next game, a three-dayer against Hampshire. It's a 90-minute trip – just enough time to watch a video called The Burning. Not a bad flick. A lot of blood and guts. [I don't know whether that was the reason for Merv's assessment or a simple statement of fact. – IC]

Get to hotel about 6.30 pm. Rooming with Maysie. Listen to some music for a while, then go to a nearby pub for dinner with AB, Cracka, Ziggy and Tugga. Home about 10.30.

Australia 5/388 (D. Martyn 138 not out, M. Slater 111, M. Hayden 98) and 6/233 dec. (M. Waugh 84, M. Taylor 57) d. Combined. Universities 7/298 dec. (S. Warne 3/45) and 157 (B. Julian 3/57, T. Zoehrer 3/16).

Saturday 26 June: Southampton

First game for me since the second Test as we meet Hampshire. AB wins the toss, we bat and declare an hour before stumps with the score on 7/393. Babs gets 160-odd and Unit 85. Hampshire go in and make 2/71. I get the two wickets. One them is David Gower who makes eight and doesn't do his Test chances any good.

[The Gower question was one of the most frequent topics of discussion in England during the Test series. The majority of media experts thought he should be in the Test team while just about every English cricket fan I encountered asked, 'Do you think Gower should be in our side?' I always answered in the affirmative, pointing out that Australian fans were, in fact, relieved to see Gower was not playing. This led English cricket fans to respond, 'And we're happy that Jones isn't playing for Australia. We can't believe they left him out.' – IC]

Back to hotel. On the way, drop most of the boys off at the pier as they are going to the Isle of Wight for a barbecue. I give it a miss and head out for a pizza. Go for a walk after and have a drink at a couple of hotels. No names, but one of them is arguably the worst pub in the world.

Sunday 27 June: Southampton

For the second time this tour, Robin Smith smashes a big hundred against us. He gets 191 out of Hampshire's 5/374 declared.

[Smith's innings included 32 fours and 4 sixes , one of which landed on the roof of the press box. David Gower, who was in the box at the time, was seen leaning out of the window trying to catch the ball as it rolled off the roof. Not to be outdone, Merv climbed the fence and sat in the crowd waiting for another mighty swipe to clear the boundary. The Hampshire fans lapped it up. – IC]

Mr Merv Hughes
Lord's Cricket Ground
London
England

To Merv Hughes
   I love Cricket and watching you on TV just <u>makes me</u> sick!
   You are the uglyist fat slob I have ever seen playing. You are an absolute 'nut' the way you carry on after getting a wicket and as far as spitting in NZ, it was the pits. You should have had a hefty <u>fine</u>!
   Listening to you speak you can tell you haven't 2 brains in your whole head. Also S. Warne - if he doesn't get every decision (oh, he is carrying on like a spoilt kid), why don't you wake up to yourselves - and grow up. You're representing Australia!!

MH
Melbourne
Australia

Back to the hotel for a few beers. Order room service and have it delivered to the bar – spaghetti with chili sauce and soup. BJ, Marto, Babs wander in after going out for a feed and we have a few more beers. Bed about midnight.

Rooming with Tim May is an entertaining experience. He's a very funny man who enjoys playing with his new toy – a remote-controlled stereo sound system. Being of the same vintage, we're both big fans of Mental As Anything and Sweet. I've got CDs by both bands and we get them pumping loud.

The Mentals are my all-time favourite band. Playing the CD reminds me of the time back in 1985 when I went to the Gold Coast with my mate Snappa. We got talking to the boys in the band and discovered they were heading north – just like us. We ended up seeing them again in Brisbane, on the Sunshine Coast, in Rockhampton and Cairns. Good value.

Monday 28 June: Southampton

Third and last day of Hampshire game. We bat until lunch and declare. Unit gets a ton and I make 61 not out.

[Anything Smith could do, Merv could do better! That was the story as Merv belted seven 6s in a truly swashbuckling innings. His competition with Craig McDermott to see who could hit the most sixes on the tour had been cancelled because of McDermott's stomach ailment, so Merv appeared to be taking on all-comers. – IC]

We set them 291 to win and they're looking good at 0/160, but we claim five wickets in six overs and the match turns into a tame draw. I get two wickets to finish the game reasonably happy.

Jump on bus to Nottingham where the third Test starts on Thursday. The boredom of the four-hour drive is broken by a couple of videos – The Hand That Rocks the Cradle and Terminator 2 – and a stop at McDonald's.

A bit of talk on the bus about England's batting order for the Test.

[Good to know that cricket wasn't forgotten amid the video viewing and Big Mac munching! England selectors, led by Lord Ted Dexter, had swung the axe after the second Test loss. Five changes saw Hick, Gatting, Lewis, Foster and Tufnell make way for Lathwell, Thorpe, Hussain, McCague and Illot. The experts were tipping England to play seven batsmen with Gooch dropping down the list. This would allow the talented young Lathwell to open with Atherton. – IC]

Australia 7/393 dec. (D. Boon 146, M. Hayden 85) and 7/271 dec. (M. Hayden 115, M. Hughes 61 not out) v. Hampshire 5/374 dec (R. Smith 191, M. Hughes 3/60) and 6/220. Match drawn.

Mr Allan Border
Ausi Captain
c/- Trent Bridge Cricket Ground
Nottingham

Dear Sir
    In the last two Tests, we saw some of the finest spin bowling ever.
    We also saw the biggest idiot ever. Please take him on one side and tell him to stop making a bloody fool of himself. He should be in a circus.

Anon.

Tuesday 29 June: Nottingham

*Train at Trent Bridge in the morning. A good session.
Fairly short because Simmo and the boys are playing golf.
Have some treatment on the knee which forces me to
miss fielding practice – what a bummer!*

*Back to hotel. Have room-service lunch, then head back to
Trent Bridge to shoot some TV ads for Telecom Australia.
[Merv was just one of many high-profile Australians who
appeared in commercials for either Telecom or Optus at the
height of the telecommunications advertising war. Very
good he was, too. – IC]*

*Spend the afternoon with Sue, then back to the hotel
for a fines meeting at seven o'clock. Also some talk about
using Duke balls in this Test instead of Reader balls.
Whatever the difference we'll go for the one which scuffs up
quicker to suit the spinners – no thought for the fast
bowlers – as usual!*

Go out for Italian dinner with Sue.

Wednesday 30 June: Nottingham

*Usual early start for training gets put on hold because
England have first use of nets. Go down to ground
anyway for warm-up and fielding practice, then into nets.
Boys work hard until training finishes about 1 pm. Get
some treatment on my knee.*

*Walk around to see Sue at her hotel. Catch a bus into city
centre for lunch, then back to team hotel for a sleep. Get up
and have some more treatment on the knee. Go to team
meeting at 6.30 where there's more talk about the England*

team and the balls. Out for a team dinner at an Italian place not far from the hotel. Good food.

MERV'S build-up to the third Test was complete – and so was mine. I'd even donned the creams myself in the break between Lord's and Trent Bridge, so I was available to do a Dirk Wellham or a Mike Whitney if required. Mind you, my form in my one and only outing was hardly headline-grabbing stuff. I didn't bat and I didn't bowl, which means, yes, all I did was field. And I didn't do that very well.

Still, I could say I'd played a game of cricket just as I could say I'd been to Lord's. Both had been long-time ambitions and I'd landed the double in the space of 10 days. It would have been sooner except for a short expedition across the English Channel to Paris straight after the Lord's Test. Three days of old buildings, crazy traffic and sky-high prices – not to mention language difficulties – were enough for me. I couldn't wait to get back to the wide open spaces of England.

The only trouble was that I couldn't say I had played cricket in England because the match was actually in Scotland. On the weekend before the Trent Bridge Test I put the pressures of Paris behind me and drove up through the pleasant countryside to Greenock, a city with a population of about 60,000 and situated half an hour west of Glasgow. The local cricket club was playing host to the Crusaders, a touring team from Victoria and South Australia led by colourful Victorian cricket identity Swan Richards. The weekend promised lashings of warm hospitality and a dash of cricket in the true spirit of the game.

I received an early indication that the promise would be fulfilled when I arrived in Greenock on the Saturday afternoon before the game and couldn't find my hotel. Coming to the end of what I thought was the right street, I saw a high red-brick wall fitting the description of the one that I'd been told surrounded Glenpark, home of the Greenock Cricket Club. Sure enough, I'd missed the pub but found the cricket ground. I wandered in through a narrow gate and saw a beautiful green arena laid out in front of me. It was set off against a backdrop of the brick wall, the inside of which was painted white. A match was in progress on the pitch nearest the pavilion which overlooked the action from atop an embankment.

Inside the pavilion, a half a dozen locals were gathered at the bar and the air was full of happy chatter and thick Scottish accents. A woman behind the bar asked if she could help me. I said, 'Yes, if you can tell me how to get to the Tontine Hotel.' A friendly chap immediately spun around, introduced himself as the club president and told me he could give me the directions. 'But first,' he said, 'you must have a drink.' I thanked him, but passed on the offer. He looked at me quizzically as did his friends. I paused for a moment and remembered the old saying, 'When in Rome, do as the Romans do; when in Scotland, have a drink.'

Sitting in the comfy chairs watching the seconds finish off their game, president Roger told me how much the locals were looking forward to the Sunday social fixture with the Crusaders. 'We had a disco last night and there's a traditional Scottish dance tonight,' he enthused. 'It's not every day we get a bunch of Aussies up here.' It sounds a bit more Irish than Scottish because the good folk of Greenock were the only ones doing the celebrating – the Aussies didn't arrive until Sunday and so missed the disco and the dance! Not that the Greenock lads were concerned. They skipped, tripped and jigged their way around the dance floor on the Saturday night in what they regarded as a perfect preparation for a social game. As for me, well, after doing the Highland fling, I was all flung out.

The Sunday dawned fine and sunny. It was simply a perfect day for cricket. When the Crusaders rolled in to Glenpark, I offered my services as 12th man, a position which I believe has become a specialist one and for which I had prepared thoroughly. I had spent many months learning the signals which players direct to the dressing room to let the 12th man know they want anything from a new bat to a helmet to a jumper to a glass of water with two level teaspoons of energy replacement powder stirred three times in a clockwise direction and allowed to settle for 26 seconds.

It was then that big Barry from Bendigo said he was happy to have a rest and invited me to take his place in the XI. This was indeed a thrill. Anyway, to cut a long story short, we batted first and made 211 for the loss of five wickets whereupon the innings was closed. Afternoon tea was taken in an old wooden hall quite separate from the pavilion with the players of both sides enjoying the get-together. It was hard to imagine the Australians and the West Indians sitting down like this for a scone and a cup of tea in the Caribbean in 1991.

Greenock began the chase steadily and kept the scoreboard ticking over at the required five runs per over. It wasn't a difficult task thanks to some short boundaries. I found out just how short the boundaries were when I chased a ball to the rope at extra cover and found myself running over the rope with the ball before I had time to pull up. I thus gave away four runs, a costly error in a tight game, and an embarrassing one because it happened right in front of the pavilion.

While talking about the boundaries, I must mention that there was a local rule which said that if a shot cleared the boundary rope on the full it was only four and not six. To score six, the ball had to clear the brick wall. A few years ago, Gordon Greenidge was the club professional and he managed to regularly smash the ball over the wall with ease. When a benefit match was staged for him, his fellow West Indians Clive Lloyd, Desmond Haynes, Brian Lara and Keith Arthurton were among a star-studded line-up gracing Glenpark for the day. On that occasion, several children were stationed in the streets to fetch the ball and they were kept very busy.

Back to our game and the equation got down to this: Greenock needed five to tie and six to win with one over remaining. The last two batsmen were at the wicket and we needed to get one of them out otherwise, under the conditions of play, the match would be a draw. Although I had made myself available to bowl at various stages of the Greenock innings, acting skipper David Emerson had overlooked me and he wasn't about to bring me on for these last six crucial deliveries. The task befell a left-arm spinner named Ian Woolf, who had bowled unchanged for about a dozen overs.

The pressure was on as Woolfie wheeled down the first ball of the over to Charlie, a Greenock veteran, who took one step down the track and smashed the ball over the rope at long off. It would have been six anywhere else, but local rules are local rules and it was only four. Still, with five balls left and just two needed for victory, you'd have to say Greenock had shortened somewhat in the betting. The odds became even shorter when Charlie stroked the next ball into the covers and took a single. The scores were level. Four balls remained and just one run would give victory to the home side.

Charlie's young batting partner, whom we shall call Jimmy, nervously took block, Woolfie pitched up the third ball of the over and it spun past the edge of the bat. A dot ball. Three left, one run to get. Ball number four was a replay of the third. Young Jimmy, his feet anchored to the crease, lunged at the ball and missed again. Two to come, one run to get. The field was placed with great care and I can remember thinking, no, praying that the ball wasn't hit in my direction. Woolfie sent down the penultimate delivery and Jimmy missed a third time. It was unbelievable stuff.

Emo called the field up for the last ball because it was obvious the batsmen would run even if the youngster missed again. In the excitement and confusion they might have been able to pinch a run. Woolfie trotted up, rolled his arm over and the batsman took an almighty swing. This time he connected. For a moment, I could see the ball flying towards me at short midwicket. Suddenly, I realised it had taken a thick outside edge and it was looping towards the slips where one of our team grabbed the catch. The last man was out and the scores were tied on 211. You couldn't have wished for a more exciting – or better – finish than that.

Was this an omen for the third Test at Trent Bridge?

6 Trouble at Trent Bridge

THE stage was set for a fascinating Test match at Trent Bridge with the Australians keen to push on to a 3–0 lead. Meanwhile, the only push that England supporters seemed interested in was the one to remove Lord Ted Dexter from his position as chairman of selectors. For this Test at least, Dexter and his co-selectors made some changes, bringing in new batsmen Mark Lathwell, Graham Thorpe and Nasser Hussain.

However, the most interesting – and controversial – selection was that of fast bowler Martin McCague. Born in Ireland, McCague moved to Australia with his parents at the age of two. Despite his birthplace and recent time in English county cricket, most people regarded him as an Aussie because of his upbringing. And that's without mentioning his cricket schooling at the Australian Cricket Academy, his representation in the Australian Under-19 team, his experience with Western Australia in the Sheffield Shield competition or a pronounced Australian drawl to his accent. His inclusion in the England team at Trent Bridge, more than any other selection for the summer, appeared to put some 'needle' into the series.

Thursday 1 July: Trent Bridge

Gooch wins the toss and bats which surprises us as we all thought they would bowl. It's a mixed first day starting with a dog on the field holding up play while I'm preparing to bowl the first ball.

We pick up Lathwell and Atherton in the first session, but Smith and Stewart bat really well after that to reach 2/153 when Warnie gets Stewart caught by Junior at cover off a half-tracker. BJ follows up with a great caught and bowled to get Smith off a full toss. Gooch, Hussain and Caddick combine to get England to 6/276 by stumps. I get three wickets, Warnie two and BJ one.

Meet Sue in the hospitality tent, then go out for a feed. For the fourth night in a row, it's Italian. There's a big group at dinner including Warnie's parents, Keith and Brigitte, and Terry 'TJ' Jenner. TJ has played a big role in Warnie's career and is on hand to pass on a few more tips.

Thursday 1 July: Trent Bridge

It took a couple of days at a friend's farm in the country to recover from the rigours of the match at Greenock. So slow was my recovery that I was late hitting the road to Nottingham, home of the famous Trent Bridge cricket ground. This meant I heard the first session on radio, an entertaining way to pass the time in the car but not quite the same as being there. This point was driven home to me when it was reported that England had won the toss and had decided to bat.

I was going to miss the first ball of the day being

delivered by Merv. And on a wicket which was likely to give some assistance to the quick bowlers, anything could happen. It did. A dog wandered on to the field. The BBC's octogenarian commentator Brian Johnston was at the microphone at the time and his description of events was marvellous stuff especially when Merv went down on all fours to eyeball the wayward mutt. Mesmerised by Merv's stare, the dog was scooped up by a member of the ground staff. Meanwhile, 'Jonners' sounded sorry to see it go. He said, 'Well, I hope that's not the last we see of the little doggie today.' He would have been disappointed to learn that the six-month-old collie cross was carted off to the local RSPCA shelter.

It's a story with a happy ending as a week later the dog was 'adopted' by an English couple named Graham and Sally Bosnall. They were among more than 60 people who offered a home for the stray pooch. A sixty-first bid was almost made by a Mr and Mrs Merv and Sue Hughes, but they ruled it out after deciding they didn't want to put the dog through 24 hours in a box on a plane, not to mention a spell in quarantine. Oh, and the name given to the dog by the Bosnalls? Merv, of course!

One other interesting observation about the BBC's morning commentary was the enthusiasm Mark Lathwell's debut as an opening batsman generated among their number. The English, of course, were looking for any sort of bright spot in an otherwise gloomy recent Test record, but the wraps on Lathwell bordered on over-the-top. Talk about putting pressure on the boy! At 11.33 am, the inevitable occurred – Merv enticed a big drive from Lathwell, who forgot to move his feet, and Ian Healy accepted a catch from the edge of the youngster's bat.

Play was well into the second session by the time I

arrived at Trent Bridge, a ground with a completely different atmosphere to Lord's. There is a much more working-class, down-to-earth feel about the place. Sure, they have a 'members only' pavilion, but it was a far cry from the jacket, tie and stiff upper lip of Lord's. In fact, on one occasion, I saw a bloke in shorts and a singlet walk straight into the pavilion under the nose of an official who didn't bat an eyelid. And what about the nearest pub? Unlike the Lord's Tavern, which is next door to Lord's, at Trent Bridge the pub is actually inside the ground.

The ticket provided by Merv again put me in among the wives, girlfriends, families and friends of the Australian players and I felt very much at home. The camaraderie extended to an invitation from Shane Warne's father Keith to take tea and scones at an afternoon function in the dining-room of the new grandstand which had been opened that day. Such was the spread that the players were back on the field before I'd started on my second scone. Anyway, our table was right near a window so we decided to watch a bit of the action from this excellent vantage point.

Not long after tea, Merv managed to get a ball to rear awkwardly and Gooch popped up a catch to Border and the England score stood at 6/220. This was the signal for the defeatist attitude of the English cricket supporter to be heard yet again as one of the locals sharing afternoon tea with us turned to his friend and said, 'We'll be lucky to get 250 now.'

I adjourned from the table and returned to my seat on the fence at fine leg, figuring it was a good time to snap a few more photos of Merv. As soon as I had him in focus, I called out to Merv to make sure he looked at the camera. Not content with simply looking in my direction, Merv decided to brighten up the picture with a hand gesture or two. To be accurate, it was a finger action rather than a hand gesture. Chuckling to myself, I clicked merrily away, but it appeared that some of the English supporters couldn't see the funny side. They must have thought Merv was having a go at them and a spate of tut-tutting broke out around me. Thank goodness it wasn't Lord's.

Dear Mr Hughes

Please find enclosed a photograph of yourself with 'Merv the Swerve'. Myself and my family are now his new owners, as you may have seen in the press.

I thought I could presume upon your good nature and ask you to sign the photograph for me. If this is possible, could you please make it out to my daughters, Charlotte and Amy.

Thank you for your time

Graham Bosnall
Horsley Village
Derby

Mr Merv Hughes
Australian
Trent Bridge
Nottingham
England

Merv
   I've seen many Tests but your running out of the cheat Atherton at Lord's was the highlight of them all (Wasim & Waqar scoring 40 odd runs to beat the Poms at Lord's last year was my no. 1 up to last Sunday).
   You may not have taken a wicket in the 2nd innings but your will to win - enthusiasm and help to Allan and the other bowlers was brilliant - but to run out the cheat - already morally out 3 times - on 99 broke his heart and filled ours with joy. Please do him at Trent Bridge a pair.
   A 100,000 Welcomes to Ireland.

Anon.
Bale Atha Claith
Ireland

Friday 2 July: Trent Bridge

We bowl England out for 321. I finish with five wickets, Warnie three and Maysie and BJ one each. Good catches by Tugga in the gully to get rid of Thorpe and BJ to get Smith. Tubby and Slats take us to lunch without loss, then it's 2/124 at tea. Babsie and Junior show the way.

Lose four wickets after tea while adding another 150-odd. The order is changed a bit because AB can't bat due to an eye infection and a virus. Cove calls round to the rooms so spend a bit of time catching up on the diary.

After play meet the girls in the Cornhill tent. Go out for dinner at an Italian place. Walk Sue home then catch a taxi back to our pub about midnight.

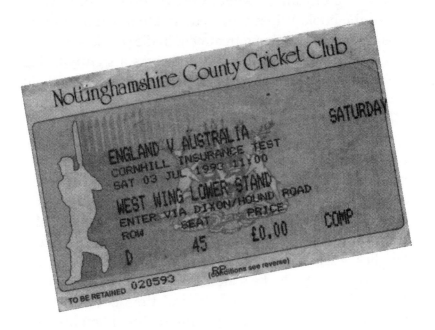

Friday 2 July: Trent Bridge

For the past 15 years, the Australian cricket team has been coming in to my lounge room every summer, but I've never been in to their rooms. Funny that. Since the so-called Packer Revolution, the television coverage of the cricket has produced all sorts of developments – cameras at both ends of the pitch, slo-mo replays from dozens of angles, stump-cam and so on. But viewers really haven't been taken any closer to the players in an off-field sense. The rooms have remained a sanctuary. We see the players on the balcony, but the cameras always seem to stop there.

At Trent Bridge, the mysteries of the Australian dressing rooms were revealed to me for the first time. On the second day, when Australia began batting after dismissing England, I went to the rooms to talk to Merv about the book. When I arrived, an attendant said Merv was downstairs receiving treatment in the physio's room so I headed down there. On the door was a sign with big letters saying 'Knock and WAIT'. I got the message and did exactly that. From the other side of the door, I recognised Merv's voice saying, 'Yeah, come in.'

I pushed the door open and came face to face with a man in cricket creams lying on a rubdown table. The only trouble was that it wasn't Merv. It was the Australian captain Allan Border. He looked tired and irritable and I feared that my knocking on the door had woken him from an afternoon nap. 'Sorry, I was looking for Merv Hughes,' I said hurriedly, not wanting to incur the wrath of the skipper. 'Yeah, he's here,' Border said, motioning across the room. I glanced around the door and there was Merv on the next table getting treatment on his knee from Errol Alcott. Later, the news broke that Border was suffering from conjunctivitis which explained his looking tired and irritable.

Merv had arranged for Tim Zoehrer to hand over the diary if I called into the dressing rooms, so he sent me upstairs to collect it. Even though I'd met the players at the farewell dinner, I must admit to being a trifle nervous about entering their inner sanctum. After all, they were in the middle of playing a Test match against England, a cricket contest that produces plenty of pressure.

However, I quickly discovered that there was a relaxed atmosphere in the rooms.

Perhaps it was the television tuned to the tennis at Wimbledon where Pete Sampras was locked in a semi-final battle with Boris Becker; perhaps it was the ghettoblaster on top of the TV belting out heavy metal music; or perhaps it was the messy confusion of clothing, cricket bats, drinks, sandwiches, newspapers, bags and equipment. Whatever, the Australian dressing room and the blokes who inhabited it combined to present a happy scene.

Out on the field that morning, the Australians had dismissed the last four England batsmen including Martin McCague who was playing against some of his former Australian Under-19 teammates. Merv greeted McCague's arrival at the wicket with a customary bouncer, but he was adamant that there was nothing personal in it. 'The Western Australian boys might have been touched a bit by his selection, but basically it was fine by us. He's qualified to play for England and if he's good enough to play for them, good luck to him,' Merv said later.

Saturday 3 July: Trent Bridge

Day three of the Test. We resume about 60 runs behind with four wickets in hand. The aim is to push on and build a handy lead, but we lose a couple of early wickets – BJ and Babs – and we're still 20 behind. AB gets 30-odd, I make 17 and Warnie bats well for 35 not out to put us 50 in front.

Things go well when we get Atherton early, but Smith gets among the runs again. By stumps, England are 4/122 with

Gooch and Caddick (nightwatchman) not out. Gooch is the key. If we are to win the match, we have to get Gooch early on Monday.

Meanwhile, we've got a rest day tomorrow and Cracka and Heals have taken the opportunity to organise a big dinner tonight. Hop in a taxi with Sue, Warnie and Simone and head for the place. It's miles away, way out of Nottingham. The roll call is Heals and Helen, Tugga and Lynette, BJ and Jackie, Cracka and Sal, Slats and Steph, Warnie and Simone, Pistol and Janet, Sue and myself. A good night.

Saturday 3 July: Trent Bridge

Someone once said that you've made the big time in Australia if you are the subject of a story on '60 Minutes'. And after the first two Tests in England, Shane Warne had certainly made the cricket big time. To cap it all off, Jeff McMullen, one of the globe-trotting reporters from '60 Minutes', rolled up at Trent Bridge with a producer and camera crew in tow to put together a story about the leg-spinning sensation.

And as soon as they arrived, they were able to get some good footage of Warne in action – with the bat rather than the ball as he helped Australia to a first innings lead. Later, when England batted a second time, the '60 Minutes' cameraman lurked near the fence at fine leg to capture shots of Warne in the field. What a shame, I thought, that they hadn't been here a couple of days earlier to film Merv giving me those colourful salutes!

While the presence of the people from '60 Minutes'

had provided some supplementary action, the real highlights were still produced by the men on the field. And heading the list was David Boon. Having finally recorded his first Test century in England in the previous Test at Lord's, Boon helped himself to back-to-back tons. Resuming at 88 not out, he sat back and waited for the loose balls which could be cracked to the boundary. They came along soon enough and Boon went 92, 96, 100. Just like that.

It's simple really. Boon's assessment – shared by everyone in cricket – was that the England bowlers were not going to be in the same class as the West Indies. But that didn't mean you could just go out there and smash everything. There would still be five good deliveries an over. Therefore, the secret to the Boon approach was to have the concentration and patience to wait for that one bad ball an over to come and then to despatch it for four. This meant that Boon's 100 at Trent Bridge, while not being a swashbuckling effort, still included 15 boundaries.

In a revealing contrast, Mark Waugh, who shared an entertaining partnership with Boon, scored 70 off 68 deliveries before being caught in the deep trying to hit Peter Such out of the ground. He had already received his 'gift' ball that over, but he wasn't prepared to wait for the next loose one. Fair dinkum, with a touch of Boon's patience, he could have made 200. Waugh knew it, too. I was in the Australian dressing rooms when he returned to the pavilion after being dismissed and he was clearly annoyed with himself. For 15 minutes, he sat in an adjoining room, still wearing his pads and repeating to himself, over and over, just one solitary word of admonition . . .

Sunday 4 July: Trent Bridge

Rest day. You beauty! What a great day! Sleep in until midday. Go downstairs for some lunch. Go around to Sue's place and watch some TV and snooze until about 4 pm.

Catch a taxi back to team hotel and go back to bed. Sleep, watch TV. Get some room service. Watch a couple of movies, then sleep. Great day.

Tourist Information *i*

Sunday 4 July: Trent Bridge

Rest days might be all right for big fast bowlers, but we spectators find them totally boring. I mean, what was there to do in Nottingham on a Sunday? Go and look at a tree where Robin Hood and his Merry Men hid from the Sheriff of Nottingham? No thanks, I'd come all this way to see Allan Border and his Happy Fellas making sure that Graham Gooch and his Sorry Side had nowhere to hide.

The sporting interest for the day was provided by the men's singles final at Wimbledon between Jim Courier and Pete Sampras. An all-American affair being played on 4 July – American Independence Day – was tailor-made for the British tabloids. Typically, they found it difficult to say anything nice and went for headlines such as 'Bored on the Fourth of July'. The BBC radio coverage, like the cricket commentary, provided colourful listening in the car on my return to London as, unfortunately, my time in England was running out after watching three days of absorbing cricket at Trent Bridge.

Monday 5 July: Trent Bridge

Fourth day of Test. BJ gets Caddick after about an hour. Caddick has been a worry to us with the bat – not making runs, but occupying the crease for long periods. Then Gooch and Thorpe put on a big partnership. Finally get Gooch in the last session, caught by Tubby off Warnie.

I do my groin halfway through the second session and don't bowl for rest of the day. Don't know how bad it is – we'll have to wait and see how it comes up in the morning.

Sue goes to London to pick up her sister Liz so I head back to the hotel, then out with Babs, Heals and Hooter to a night for a group of Australians who are over here on a tour. Not a bad night.

Monday 5 July: London

While the action resumed at Trent Bridge, I was running around London with BBC radio as my link to the cricket. It was one of those days where you pop in and out of the car and hear only snatches of the commentary. After a while, I worked out that Gooch was still going and Thorpe was giving him great support. However, amid all the mentions of Gooch and Thorpe, the name Hughes seemed to have disappeared. The mystery was unravelled when one of the commentators talked about Hughes being off the ground because of an injury.

At first I feared that Merv had suffered a recurrence of his knee trouble, but it turned out to be a groin problem this time. Merv was sending down the fourth delivery of his 22nd over of the innings when he felt a twinge. 'I knew something was wrong so I came straight off for some treatment,' Merv said later. 'I thought it might free up after tea so I went back on to the ground to give it a test. It was no good so I came off for more treatment.'

Merv's exit from the attack meant Australia's fast bowling stocks had taken a nose-dive with Craig McDermott already out of business for the series. McDermott was at Trent Bridge to say goodbye to his teammates before heading home to Queensland to recuperate. Hopefully, Merv wouldn't be going with him.

Tuesday 6 July: Trent Bridge

The groin feels OK when I get up in the morning. A bit tight, but not as bad as I thought it would be. There's no way I'll bowl, though, so I sit back and watch Thorpe and Hussain make some quick runs. Thorpe gets a hundred and England declare midway through the first session, leaving us 371 to win. The target is out of the question, so it's just a matter of the boys batting out the day. At lunch, we're going well at 0/40.

Things get a bit wobbly in the next session as we slip to 6/120 at tea. Heals falls last ball before the break and things go pretty quiet in the rooms. The tension is fairly high, but BJ, who is batting with Tugga, looks so relaxed it's almost unbelievable. It's five o'clock before the rest of us loosen up. We don't lose a wicket after tea with Tugga and BJ doing a great job.

We're happy with a draw and the England boys also

look happy with the result. I find that surprising because if we'd been in their position at tea, we'd have been disappointed not to go on and win.

Tuesday 6 July: London

As I was heading back to Australia the next day, I figured that a day on the couch watching the cricket would help me get my strength up for the gruelling flight home. This idea was aborted during the morning when it was deemed that there was still some last-minute shopping to do. And, my wife reminded me, we hadn't seen the Changing of the Guard and this was our last chance. I said the only changing of the guard I wanted to see was Lord Ted Dexter handing over the reins as England's chairman of selectors, a point on which I had total support from English supporters.

A taxi tooted out the front and we were off to Buckingham Palace just as Gooch made the declaration. I would have to rely on overhearing radio descriptions as we moved around for the day, but that proved to be easier said than done. Eventually, I picked up an afternoon paper and was shocked to see the Australians were struggling after lunch. When I read that Border was one of the not-out batsman, I relaxed in the knowledge that he had a fine track record in this sort of backs-to-the-wall situation.

A couple of hours later, we were all shopped out and I suggested we should go home to watch the last session on television. Jumping in to a taxi, my nerves were set on edge again when the driver relayed the news of Healy's dismissal from the last ball before tea. I tried to pretend I wasn't interested in the cricket, but the driver's confidence had soared after hearing Andrew Caddick take three quick, top-order wickets. 'Get out of it,' he said, 'I can tell you're here for the cricket and you're not happy that we're going to beat you today.'

London boasted thousands of taxis. When it came to cricket, the drivers fell into three categories: those who followed it closely, those with a passing interest, and those with no interest whatsoever. On this day, I would have been happy to strike a driver from either of the last two categories, but it was my luck to cop one from the first group. Make no mistake, he was an expert. Within five minutes, he'd sacked almost the entire England team because of their general lack of ability. Strange as it seemed, he also believed that this same hopeless bunch was good enough to beat Australia as we spoke.

I got home in time to see Steve Waugh and Brendon Julian steering Australia to safety while, somewhere in London, a taxi driver was trying to work out whether Australia was lucky to get out of the Test with a draw or if England had reached new depths of hopelessness.

Australia 373 (D. Boon 101, M. Waugh 70; M. McCague 4/121, M. Illot 3/108) and 6/202 (B. Julian 56 not out; A. Caddick 3/32) v. England 321 (R. Smith 86, N. Hussain 71; M. Hughes 5/92, S. Warne 3/74) and 6/422 dec. (G. Gooch 120, G. Thorpe 114 not out, R. Smith 50; S. Warne 3/108). Match drawn. Man of the Match: Graham Thorpe.

Dear Merv
  Just a note to say how lovely it was yesterday seeing you being so kind and thoughtful to the little dog that ran out on the pitch.
  Obviously being English I would like to see England win, but now I shall not feel so bad if Australia wins after seeing your act of kindness.

Good luck.

P.H. (Mrs)
Cheshire

Dear Merv Hughes
  This is a sort of fan letter. Not so much re. your great cricketing prowess - but about the lovely way you dealt with that dog at Trent Bridge. Brilliant the way you got down to his level - eyeball to eyeball. I saw it on TV and then the super picture on the front of the Daily Telegraph.
  Thanks so much and for being a great cricketer, too.

Yours sincerely

MJ

THE battle was on for Merv to overcome his groin injury in time for the fourth Test starting at Headingley on 22 July. To assist the cause, it was decided that Merv should return to London for intensive treatment under the guidance of physio Errol Alcott. This meant missing out on a trip to Ireland where everyone was looking forward to a well-earned rest and a few rounds of golf. Oh, and there was the small matter of a couple of one-day games against the Minor Counties and Ireland.

Wednesday 7 July: London

Head back to London with Sue and Hooter. Hooter's plans for going to Euro Disney are up the creek because he has to stay in London to treat my strained groin. Most of the conversation centres around who is going to tell Hooter's son Adam the bad news.

Check in to the Westbury then go to the gym which is about 800 metres away. Do a pool session consisting of kicking, running in water, stretching, wet sauna and more stretching in water. Back to Hooter's room for ultrasound and differential treatment. Out for Mexican dinner with Hooter, Adam and Maysie, who's got this game off and has come to London.

Thursday 8 July: London

Get up about 10 and go to the gym with Hooter. Do a pool session then back to hotel for treatment. Grab some lunch and watch TV before going back to the gym for a workout. The workout calls for 15 minutes on the exercise bike, a set of stretching exercises and a weights circuit which seems to take eight hours. Back to hotel for more treatment. Out for dinner at Planet Hollywood.

Friday 9 July: London

Kick off the day with a pool session at 10.30 am followed by treatment in Hooter's room. Grab some lunch and watch some TV. Back to the gym for another workout. No trouble with the groin apart from a bit of stiffness. No twinges at all.

Saturday 10 July: London

Pool session in morning followed by treatment. Sue goes sightseeing, but I prefer sleeping. Get up about 1.30 pm and go to the gym for a workout. Go for a drive and grab some fish and chips for tea. Watch the movie Big starring Tom Hanks, then part of Ferris Bueller's Day Off.

[Meanwhile, Merv missed the party in Ireland where the Australians declared after smashing 3/361 off just 49.4 overs. Allan Border called a halt to the slaughter when he was dismissed for 111, made in 44 minutes off 56 balls with 10 fours and eight 6s. Five of the sixes came off consecutive deliveries in one over from a poor chap named Angus Dunlop. Remember that name. It will be the answer to a cricket trivia question one day. By the way, the home side replied with 89. – IC]

Sunday 11 July: London

Sleep in and take the morning off. Hooter takes his mother and Adam to the airport for their flight home. When Hooter gets back, we go for a pool session and a workout. Go out for Mexican dinner then back to hotel and watch Caddyshack. What a great show.

Monday 12 July: London

Last day of treatment in London before rejoining the boys. [The intensive five-day program of exercise and treatment had put Merv on the road to a full recovery for the fourth Test, according to Errol Alcott. 'He's coming along pretty well. The flexibility is good and there is no pain,' Alcott said. 'He's really exhausted because we've been working him so hard, but he's raring to go.' – IC]

Do some packing and get things sorted out as we won't be back in London until the last Test. Pack up the stuff I don't need and leave it in the store room before leaving for Derby at 3 pm. It's a two-hour drive, make that three because my navigational skills aren't too flash. We end up heading south on the A38 when we should be going north. Arrive about 6.30 pm. It's a great old English hotel situated on a golf course. Rooming with Pistol.

Tuesday 13 July: Derby

First day of three-day match against Derbyshire. The ground, which reminds me of a country showground, is a former race track and boasts a grandstand that could do with a coat of paint. I'm not playing in order to do more work on fixing the groin. Do a gym workout and a pool session with Maysie. Have lunch and get some treatment. Check to see if I can play golf, but Hooter says no.

So Maysie and myself drive to an American adventure park about half an hour out of Derby. Go on a few rides. Most of them are average, but one is a real ball-tearer. It's a cross between a roller-coaster, a corkscrew and the Big

Dipper. What's more, it goes forward, then backwards. We have to sit there showing no fear and acting cool. Manage that OK when we're going forward, but when it goes backwards, I'm hanging on like stink. What a buzz!

Back to the hotel and discover the boys going in all directions – some are off to an INXS concert in Leicester; others are heading out to a promotional night for the tour sponsor. Nothing for me, I'm having an early night. Watch some TV. Pistol gets back about 11 and gives the thumbs-up to the INXS show. He's also got a great fine ready to bring Warnie back down to earth because he reckoned the 25,000 people at the concert were there to see him when they sang the song 'Suicide Blonde'.

[By the way, some cricket was played on this day with Derbyshire making 5/244 before rain washed out play at tea. – IC]

Wednesday 14 July: Derby

Get up about 10.30 and go to the gym for a workout and pool session. Go to the ground after lunch and hear that Derbyshire were bowled out for 305 with Cracka taking five wickets including a hat-trick. Rain washes out play at tea for the second day in a row. [Australia was 1/268 at the time with Michael Slater making a dazzling unbeaten century. In doing so, he became the first player on the tour to pass 1000 runs. The young batting sensation had set himself the 1000-run target and achieved it with eight matches and 41 days to spare. – IC]

Drive AB, Ziggy, Marto and Junior back to hotel as they are going to play golf while I'm off to the gym for a workout and pool session. Have dinner with Hooter and play the poker machines for a while. A few drinks with the journos on tour before going to bed.

Thursday 15 July: Derby

Last day of game is washed out without a ball being bowled. [The rain also put paid to Australia's chances of the $100,000 bonus for winning 10 of the 14 county games. – IC] Sleep in. Pick up Marto and Unit at the ground and drive to Durham, about three hours away. Watch some of the British Open on TV.

Meet AB and Babs in the bar as we are going to dinner with Deano. [Dean Jones, overlooked for the Ashes tour, had taken up an appointment as coach of Durham seconds. – IC] Go for a pub feed then back to the hotel about 11. Watch the midnight movie called House Guests before going to sleep.

Australia 1/268 (M. Slater 133 not out, M. Waugh 60 not out) v. Derbyshire 305 (W. Holdsworth 5/117, P. Reiffel 4/82). Match drawn.

Friday 16 July: Durham

Get up and leave for optional training session at Durham University ground. As we get there, the skies open up and the rain pours down – yeah!

Go for a walk around town and get a haircut. Off to the

IAN'S SNAPS

Merv, looking like a bouncer at a high-class nightclub, asks me to show my entree card at the farewell dinner.

'It could've been me' — Matthew Hayden, flanked by his parents, watches the openers put on 260 for the first wicket at Lord's.

An historic moment at Lord's as umpire Merv Kitchen raises his finger to send Robin Smith on his way, stumped Healy bowled May. Smith became the first batsman in a Test in England to be given out via video replay.

One of the many quaint sights at Lord's — picnic baskets, cooler boxes and rugs wait for their owners to return for lunch.

An Earl's Court Roo crashes over a pack of London Hawks during a British Australian Rules Football League match near Kew Gardens. I couldn't live without a footy fix on a Saturday arvo, even in England.

The Kew Cricket Club pavilion nestles in a typical park cricket setting. Please note: members only behind the picket fence.

Me with my new-found chums (from left) Tony, Alan and Patrick in the
packed members' area on the last day of the Lord's Test match.

'Hey, Merv, get ya hands outta ya pockets!'

'Come out here and say that.'

'That's more like it.' Poetry in motion as Merv heads back to fine leg after a snappy piece of fielding.

Desperately seeking Mervyn on the hallowed turf at Lord's. The big fella is in there somewhere meeting the Queen.

'Your shout, Warnie!' The Lord's Test is over, the Aussies lead 2-0 and the celebrations are in full swing outside the Lord's Tavern.

Doing my Merv Hughes impression at fine leg during the match at Greenock.

The fake Merv mos were everywhere, even on these English blokes at Trent Bridge.

Merv leads the team off the ground at Trent Bridge after taking 5/92 in England's first innings.

Ian Chappell, who once said, 'The trouble with Merv Hughes is he thinks he's a fast bowler', tells viewers back home that Merv has just taken five wickets.

*gym and pool followed by treatment back at the hotel.
Watch the British Open on TV, then a movie.*

Merv Hughes, Esq.
c/- Australian Cricket Tour Party
'Headingley'
England

My Dear Merv
  *Sorry about your breakdown in Health. I hope that
you have recovered. You only have yourself to blame.
Charging up to the stumps like a Bull Elephant or a
Hippo looking for water. McDermott who is only half of
your weight, does the same as you. He ended up on a
plane back Home. You are now 31 years old, well
overweight and over the Hill. Reduce your run up when
bowling or you will not see this tour over. You will be on
a plane back Home. Watch yourself on the TV replays.
Ease up or we will not see you at the MCG. Enjoy the
next three Tests. Go on a diet, Merv.*

JC
Victoria
Australia

Saturday 17 July: Durham

*First day of three-day match against Durham. We lose toss
and bat. I'm sharing 12th-man duties with Slats, so head off
to the gym for the daily workout and pool session.
Durham bat all day and reach 8/385. Catch up with
Deano and spend most of the day talking to him. He
seems to be in a good frame of mind and enjoying
himself over here.*

Walk back to hotel after play. Tub up and go out for a promotional night at a sports club about a half an hour's drive away. Also on duty tonight are AB, Tugga and BJ. Big Jo Angel, who's over here playing club cricket, also comes along for a look. The function winds up about 11 and we head back to the team hotel for a few drinks in the bar. Bed about 1.30 am.

Sunday 18 July: Durham

Second day of the game. Down to the pool at 8 am for a pool session. Walk down to the ground, warm up and bowl off short run in the nets. Watch the start of play then go to the ground over the back for another net session. Bowl to Slats, Warnie and Junior. Groin feels fine and everything appears on track for the Test. Not a good day for our batsmen – we're bowled out for 221 and have to follow on.

Greg Norman wins the British Open much to the delight of the 13 Aussies watching the action on TV for most of the day. [Perhaps this explained why the batsmen were knocked over so quickly – they wanted to get back to the rooms to watch the golf! – IC]

Walk back to hotel where Cracka plays Superman in the lift and tries to open the doors between floors. Result – stuck in the lift for 20 minutes. He'll cop a fine for this, perhaps even the Daktari Suit.

Do some shots for Channel Seven and British Sky TV for about an hour then have a few beers in the bar with Cracka, Hooter and Babs. Room-service dinner and bed about 10.30.

Monday 19 July: Durham

Last day of game and rain delays start until 2.30 pm. Babs and Unit get tons and then the batting order is changed when Babs gets out. This allows Cracka to bat at second drop. AB has a 50-quid bet with him that he can't make 20. Cracka looks a chance as he hits three boundaries, but he doesn't get any further and AB collects.

The other highlight of the day comes when the crowd gives Ian Botham a standing ovation as he walks off the field at the end of the day. Many people have said it before and I'll say it again, he should have been an Australian. He plays the game like us with a very competitive approach. For all that and more, it's fitting that he plays his last first-class game against Australia because he's produced some of his greatest feats against us over the years. Durham is producing a benefit booklet to mark the occasion and I'm asked for a contribution. It's not every day that you get an opportunity to do something for a player of the calibre of Ian Botham. It's a great honour.

Jump on bus for two-hour trip to Leeds. Watch Hard to Kill. Stop for food about halfway. Get to hotel about 8.30 and have an early night. Rooming with Pistol.

Australia 221 (I. Healy 70 not out) and 3/295 (M. Hayden 151 not out, D. Boon 112) v. Durham 8/385 dec. Match drawn.

137

Tuesday 20 July: Leeds

Training at 9 am. After a talk in the rooms about the importance of this Test match, the boys train very well. [The ability to increase the intensity as a Test approached was a feature of the Australians' game. And it was just what the doctor ordered especially as their lead-up had been less than ideal with the last two county games interrupted by rain. And, for his part, Merv was picking up the tempo. – IC]

At this stage, my groin feels good. Bowl for 50 minutes off a short run-up then bowl for 15 minutes on the centre wicket. Back to hotel for some physio treatment.

The rest of the day goes like this: room-service lunch, sleep, room-service dinner. When I'm not sleeping, I'm watching MTV. Almost a perfect day.

Get a call from my sister Peta who arrived in London two days ago. She's coming to the Test. Sue also phones. She's back from a week in the Greek islands. Hard life, hey?

Wednesday 21 July: Leeds

Overnight rain leaves the ground a tad wet for training, but we go ahead anyway. Do a fairly long warm-up and then bowl for 30–40 minutes in the nets off a short run. Finish off with 10 minutes on the centre wicket. Another good session – the boys seem very keen to do well this Test.

Spend the afternoon in bed watching TV. [Regulation Test build-up for Merv. – IC] *Down to the pool for swim and stretch with BJ and Hooter. BJ is in the pool after straining his groin at training. He looks doubtful for the match.*

Up to room, shower and get dressed for team meeting.

Team not announced because of injuries and the wicket. [Traditionally, the Headingley wicket has been tinged with green, and is helpful to seam bowling. This time around, the pitch was a pale, straw colour. It looked likely to favour the batsmen, the spinners and then the seamers, in that order. When Peter Such was left out of the final XI, it appeared, however, that England still thought the seamers would prevail. – IC]

Dear Merv

I am just writing you a little note to say how great it is to watch when you are bowling. Even though I am English ('Pom'), I enjoy your snarling and your confrontations, especially with Robin Smith. It is brilliant. I was young when Lillee was in his heyday but I can remember a little bit about him and to me you are just as snarling. I also liked the look you gave Mark Illot. Just brilliant. But what impresses me about you is that you are a '100 percent' man. If England had eleven of you we would have won the Ashes by now.

Yours sincerely
NB
Dudley
West Midlands

PS. Shane Warne may get all the headlines but you are the heart and soul of the team, the Top Man.

7 Welcome to the 200 Club

ALTHOUGH down 0–2, England went into the fourth Test with renewed confidence after a vastly improved performance at Trent Bridge. The Australians, on the other hand, were looking to regain the positive approach which marked their efforts in the first two Tests. Captain Allan Border and coach Bobby Simpson spelled out the message to their charges in no-nonsense terms. 'This is the crunch Test for us,' Border said. 'We have lost a little bit of ground and we must get our enthusiasm back. At the start of the tour everyone was alert to the small points in their game. I want that edge back.'

Thursday 22 July: Headingley

This is a big match for us. England played well in the last Test and we didn't do as well as we would have liked. We've trained well for the last two days and spirits are high. It's also a big match for me after copping the groin injury, but I'm confident I'll stand up. As a bonus, we win the toss and bat which gives me even more time for treatment. Pretty happy about that.

Slats and Tubby get us off to another good start then Babs and Junior put together another good partnership. By stumps we're 3/307 with Babs and AB not out. Babs,

141

with another 100, is having a great tour.
Catch bus back to hotel, order room service and watch TV.

Thursday 22 July: Melbourne

It was hard to come home from England. You know how it is after a holiday – you don't want it to end and, when it does, it is hard to settle down again. When the fourth Test started, I simply wanted to be there.

Of course, the television coverage provided some sort of consolation and, for the first night anyway, I did it in style when I was invited to a dinner put on by a group of about 50 sports fans. This group gets together for dinner about four times a year, each with a different sporting theme. This one was a cricket night and, to add to their enjoyment, they had installed a giant video screen which made the players look life-sized.

I was seated at a table right in front of the screen. When Mark Taylor and Michael Slater came out to open the innings, I felt like I was fielding at silly mid-on. The dinner was rollicking good fun with everyone barracking as enthusiastically as they would at the ground. Slater's slashes through the off side were greeted with cheers while Martin McCague copped plenty of 'advice' whenever he was shown in close-up as he walked back to his bowling mark.

The opening stand ended at 86 when Taylor was trapped lbw by Martin Bicknell. Cries of 'rubbish', 'nowhere near it' and 'you've got to be kidding' broke out around the room. 'It didn't look out from where we were sitting,' roared the occupants of one table and you couldn't argue with them – their table was almost side-on to the big screen.

As David Boon waddled out to join Slater, another insightful observation was offered from a guest at my table. 'How'd you be if you were in the England side right now? You've finally made the breakthrough and your confidence has been given a lift. Next thing, you look up and there's Boon coming through the gate. You'd almost wish you hadn't taken the wicket.'

The story was repeated soon after when Slater, who had a century there for the taking, got too excited and was bowled for 67. The batsmen coming through the gate to replace him was Mark Waugh. With Boon, he'd figured in century partnerships in each of the first three Tests and they proceeded to help themselves to another one.

Friday 23 July: Headingley

Another big batting day. Do a fairly long warm-up followed by a session of bowling and catching then sit back and watch the runs flow. Boonie gets out early for 107, but AB and Tugga take over and bat magnificently. At the end of the day, they've both got tons and we're 4/614. What a day.

Go to gym in the rugby rooms after play and do some stretching exercises, sit-ups and four kilometres on the treadmill. Shower up then go to meet girls in the hospitality tent before heading out for dinner. Tonight's choice is Chinese. Wash it down with a pint of Coke.

A great day all round except for an altercation outside the ground in which Ziggy gets belted by three blokes while trying to get on the bus. Unfortunately, no-one else is

*around at the time. Marto rolls up just as it's clearing up
and cops one for his measure as well. Security is going to be
tightened up and the bus will be coming inside the ground in
future.*

Friday 23 July: Melbourne

The Aussie run feast seemed certain to continue with the
in-form David Boon and Allan Border at the wicket and up
against an England attack which lacked experience and
penetration. What a night for lying back on the couch
and revelling in the batting display. Alas, a social
function beckoned me away from the TV viewing.

The social event was a school fundraiser attended by
about 450 people. They were happy to be there, but most
were hoping for an early finish so they could get home to
watch the cricket. Sensing the interest in the cricket, the
master of ceremonies arranged for a helper to monitor
the radio commentary so that he could provide updates of
the scores throughout the evening.

A huge collective sigh echoed around the school hall
when it was announced that Boon had fallen lbw to Illot.
However, it was pointed out that Steve Waugh, an
unbeaten century-maker at Headingley in 1989, was
joining Border. The updates continued with news of the
Border–Waugh union pushing Australia's score past 400
and the skipper's own total nearing 100 as the function
drew to a close.

The timing was perfect. I dashed to my car which was
parked in a quiet cul-de-sac and turned on the radio to
find Border on 98. A few balls later, yet another milestone

was written into the cricket history books alongside his name. The excitement got to me and I tooted the horn gleefully whereupon the lights came on in two houses and dogs started barking. I quickly started the car and drove away.

Saturday 24 July: Headingley

AB and Tugga look like they could bat for a couple of days, but a declaration is planned for this morning which means I'll be bowling today. The end comes after an hour when AB reaches 200. Tugga is 157 not out and the partnership is worth 332.

We get an early wicket before lunch. ['We' is, in fact, Merv who has Lathwell caught by Healy from the third ball of the innings. – IC] Smith falls to spin again, this time it's Maysie claiming his wicket with a caught and bowled. Pistol gets Stewart and they're in trouble at 3/50. Gooch and Atherton build a partnership until Pistol bowls really well after tea and ends the day with five wickets.

At stumps, England are 7/195 with all their batsmen out. Pistol has an impressive haul of Atherton, Gooch, Stewart, Thorpe and Hussain. Back to the hotel and have a drink in the bar with Jamie Mitchell from Richmond Cricket Club. Up to the room about 9.30, order room service and watch TV.

Saturday 24 July: Melbourne

There was no way I was going anywhere tonight. The No. 1 attraction was seeing whether Allan Border could score 200. Not far behind at No. 2 was the fact that Merv would be back in action after his groin injury. Media reports had been talking about the new slim-line Merv and how he had shed 5kg during his intensive rehabilitation program. One story claimed Merv was 'looking as fit as he has for several seasons'.

But first things first. Allan Border was in pursuit of his double ton and, from the outset, he looked to be in no trouble whatsoever. When he glided Andy Caddick to third man after an hour's play, the skipper had his second 200 in Test cricket. In a rare display of emotion, he waved his bat several times to his teammates and the crowd, ripped off his helmet and declared the innings closed. The score stood at a mammoth 4/653, the best by any Test side at Headingley. The unfinished partnership between Border and Steve Waugh was worth 332, Waugh's contribution being 157 not out.

It was fairly safe to say Australia was in a pretty good position although a few experts feared that the innings might have continued on a fraction too long. Those fears were dispelled in the opening over of England's first innings when Merv tempted Mark Lathwell to flash at a delivery outside the off stump. Ian Healy accepted the catch and England was 1/0. In a cruel contrast, England had toiled for 193 overs without a catch while Australia picked up one after just three balls.

Lathwell's wicket took Merv's tally in Test cricket to 197 and he seemed certain to claim his 200th before this Test was finished. A week earlier, he was worried that a curse had befallen him and Craig McDermott. 'You know how batsmen go through the nervous 90s,' Merv said. 'Well, I reckon we bowlers are going through the nervous 190s. McDermott gets to 198 and he has to go home; I get to 196 and I break down.'

The late nights were taking their toll again and I battled to stay awake into the wee, small hours. Happy that I'd seen Merv make the breakthrough followed by wickets to May and Reiffel, I nodded off to sleep as Atherton and Gooch attempted to steady the sinking ship. This meant I missed the last hour in which Reiffel took four wickets in a devastating 30-ball spell. It had taken almost three days, but a seamer had once again stolen the limelight at Headingley.

Sunday 25 July: Headingley

Clean up the England innings fairly quickly and they start batting again. Lathwell and Atherton do quite well and carry England to 0/37 at lunch. By tea, they're 1/116 with Lathwell the man out. Maysie gets the wicket. He gets two more after tea as England finish the day on 4/237.

Maysie's two wickets after tea are both stumpings and they require the third umpire to make the decision. Pistol gets the other wicket when Smith is trapped in front not offering a shot.

Just for something different, catch the bus back to the hotel, order room service and watch TV.

Sunday 25 July: Melbourne

'What are you doing tonight?' a mate asked me during the day. 'Do you want to come to a party?' 'No,' I said, 'I'm having a quiet night at home watching the Australians finish off the Poms.' My mate was dumbfounded. 'I don't know how you can be bothered,' he said. 'I can't watch it any more. In fact, I'm starting to feel sorry for poor old England.' Never feel sorry for them, I thought. We've been on the end of some dreadful beatings over the years and you've got to enjoy it when the opportunity comes along.

So I settled back on the couch for another pleasant night's viewing. It didn't take long for Merv and Warnie to grab the last three wickets, leaving England all out for 200 – which was exactly the same number of runs scored by *one* Australian batsman. England was well and truly on the ropes and the Ashes were as good as in the bag. All that was required was another ten wickets and there was plenty of time to complete the job.

And Merv needed to take just one of the ten wickets to give himself 200 Test scalps. There would be no excuse if I nodded off to sleep and missed that milestone. A couple of times I succumbed. On both occasions, I woke up to discover a wicket had fallen and my heart skipped a beat as I waited for the scoreboard to come up on the TV screen after the ad breaks. A quick reading of the board revealed that May and Reiffel were the wicket-takers which meant Merv was anchored on 199.

Monday 26 July: Headingley

Start the day needing six wickets to retain the Ashes. A couple of early wickets will set us on the right road and Pistol does the job picking up Stewart and Thorpe. Stewart ends up with 78 and gives me some stick, hitting four boundaries in one over. Not happy about that.

Sitting on 199 wickets is a bit nerve-wracking, but the 200 comes when I get Caddick lbw. Don't have to wait long for the 201st as Bicknell goes next ball, also lbw. At lunch England are 8/279.

Half an hour after lunch we pick up the last two wickets that give us the Test, the series and the Ashes. Fittingly, AB takes a catch off Maysie to end the innings. It's just as well he takes it, too, because the six stumps are being souvenired while the ball is in the air.

The boys are on a high and the celebrations get into full swing in the rooms. Everyone gets drowned by flying beer, there are no exceptions. Anyone who walks into our rooms cops it. Drink a bit of it, too, as we sit around enjoying the occasion for a couple of hours.

Back at the hotel, the tour sponsors organise a room for a party with the biggest bucket of beer I've ever seen. The celebrations fire up and the young blokes are keen to go out and kick on. I'm out of steam, though, by 11.30 pm.

Tired and emotional, I go to bed.

Monday 26 July: Melbourne

Roll up, roll up for the Australian Ashes triumph. Laugh along with Allan Border as he knocks up 200. Marvel at Merv Hughes claiming his 200th Test wicket. Shed a tear as Graham Gooch steps down as England skipper.

The advertising gurus would have had a ball cranking up the promotional blurbs if they'd known the Headingley Test was going to unfold this way. Sitting back on the couch or lying in bed in Australia, it made memorable viewing. Heading my list of highlights – and that of many others – was Merv's performance.

Among those handing out the bouquets was former England opening batsman Geoffrey Boycott. In 108 Tests he played against some of the best fast bowlers in the game – except Merv. But he admitted he would not fancy batting against the newest member of the 200-wicket club.

Interviewed by Terry Brindle for a feature story in the Yorkshire Post, Boycott said of Merv, 'He's a bugger. You'd never know what to expect from him and unpredictability is an important quality in a fast bowler.'

Boycott said one of the biggest traps for a batsman was to under-estimate Merv. 'He may not look like a typical hero and he might have a reputation for being a bit of a jokey figure, but he is very professional, I've no doubt about that,' he said.

'He uses his head, this bloke. Look at the way he bowled to Alec Stewart at Lord's – slipped him a bouncer and Stewart whacked it for four, gave him another next ball, a bit higher and a bit wider. Come on, he says, hit that one, go and fetch it and you'll be in trouble. Merv knows what he's doing; he's no mug.

'The thing I like most about him is aggression, his wonderful, competitive spirit. There are people who have an abundance of talent and there are those with ability who get the best out of themselves. You can forgive a player almost anything as long as he tries and Merv always puts in 100 per cent.

'He doesn't have a classical action, he looks overweight and he turns it on a bit for the crowd, but he's got a much better cricket brain than a lot of people give him credit for.

'He'd have been regarded as no more than lively fast-medium in my day but he always bowls intelligently – like the way he always delivers the short stuff into the ribs. Nothing ballooning over the head to get the crowd excited, nothing wasted. A hard man to face.'

And an example, Boycott said, to a generation weaned off the work ethic. 'He thinks about the game, he works hard at it, he gets the best out of himself. I've always said that anyone can learn to play better. How good you actually become depends on other factors, like how much ability you were blessed with in the first place and how much you are prepared to work at it.

'From what I've seen of his attitude and ability, Merv deserves to be remembered as a very good Test bowler.'

Eight years earlier, at the start of his Test career, Merv had been branded an imposter and that stinging description fired him up. In fact, it still does. That revelation came from the man himself when he was interviewed after the Headingley Test.

'It has been a great motivation for me to succeed because of those things written early in my career about Merv Hughes, the imposter,' he said. 'You try and turn people around and hopefully I have gone a long way towards doing that over the last couple of years. You have a lot of blokes criticise you and I don't mind copping it from blokes who have played a lot.

'I have copped a bit from Ian Chappell, Jeff Thomson and Richie Benaud and I hope I have turned them around. Test cricket is a very hard game. There are not too many blokes who have been instant successes at that level. Once you get there it makes you want to be there and work harder.'

As one of those former players who had been critical, Richie Benaud had the last word on Merv's 200 Test wickets. 'It is a great performance. Early in his career, Hughes could have been a few Tests wonder, more froth and bubble than performance and the biggest problem was that he didn't seem quite sure what he wanted to do.

'It is a measure of his courage and temperament that he

soon sorted out what was required of him and for several years now he has bowled magnificently.'

Australia 4/653 (A. Border 200 not out, S. Waugh 157 not out, D. Boon 107, M. Slater 67, M. Waugh 52) d. England 200 (G. Gooch 59, M. Atherton 55; P. Reiffel 5/65, M. Hughes 3/47) and 305 (A. Stewart 78, M. Atherton 63; T. May 4/65, M. Hughes 3/79, P. Reiffel 3/87) by an innings and 148 runs. Man of the Match: Allan Border.

The Australian 200 Club

Bowler	Test Matches	Wickets	Average
Dennis Lillee	70	355	23.9
Richie Benaud	63	248	27.0
Graham McKenzie	61	246	29.8
Ray Lindwall	61	228	23.0
Clarrie Grimmett	37	216	24.2
Merv Hughes	51	208	27.7
Jeff Thomson	51	200	28.0

Dear Merv

My name is Sonia. I am 6 years old. I like watching cricket and I am a great fan of you and the Aussies.

I would be very grateful if you would send me a picture of you and your team with your autographs. I have got a picture of you on your motorbike with a gun. You look like Arnie.

Yours sincerely
Miss Sonia M.
Wolverhampton

Hello Merv

I read an article in the paper on Friday stating that you have a love–hate relationship with the crowd. You love 'em, they hate you. Speaking for myself, I don't hate you, mate. I think you are one of the all-time best fast bowlers and a truly great cricket character in the mould of one of my all-time favourites, Fred Trueman.

Being a Yorky I associate myself with you Aussies. I hate losing and can't stand whingers. I would very much appreciate a signed photo of yourself if you can find the time.

Hope you have a long and successful career. All the best to you and the Aussie team, Merv.

Sincerely
MB
PS. Wish you were English and a Yorky.

Tuesday 27 July: Headingley to Manchester

The boys look a tad weary when they assemble in the hotel foyer before boarding the bus bound for Manchester. Well, you don't win the Ashes every day, do you? Watch Major League on video then stop for lunch. Reach Manchester about 2 pm, book in, then go out with Slats, Marto and Unit to see Jurassic Park. Not a bad show.

The papers are full of tributes to Graham Gooch. They all say he's a great player and what a pity it is that he has decided to stand down as captain. I can't understand this because they have been bagging him for the last two months and saying that he's got to go. Unbelievable. There's also plenty of speculation about who is going to take over as the next England captain. Atherton, Stewart and Gatting are leading the bunch.

Wednesday 28 July: Manchester

First day of three-day game against Lancashire at Old Trafford and, more importantly, my wife's birthday. Do warm-up, but play is delayed because the ground is wet. I have never seen so much interest in the toss – not too many blokes are keen to field or bowl today. We win the toss and bat. Everyone loves our acting captain Tubby Taylor. [He's pretty happy with himself, too, as he notches a century. – IC]

Thursday 29 July: Manchester

Warm up for the second day's play with a game of touch rugby between the Nerds and the Julios. Nerds go down 5–2. Straight into the field as we declare on the overnight score of 3/282. Lancashire, in turn, declare at 7/250 with Warnie getting another three wickets.

BJ isn't playing this game, but he still makes a great contribution with a classic one-liner at lunch. Observing how the Lancashire batsmen were playing and missing, he says, 'These blokes couldn't nick a TV in the LA riots.'

Back to hotel then out to see Jurassic Park again and it's just as good the second time around.

154

Friday 30 July: Manchester

Last day of Lancashire game. We bat until just after lunch and declare at 8/194, leaving Lancashire 227 to win off 55 overs. We end up bowling 61 with Maysie and Warnie sending down 49 between them. Lancashire get up by hitting six off the second ball of the last over. Young opener John Crawley – we call him 'Creepy' – makes 100 and bats pretty well.

After game, drive to Glamorgan with Pistol at the wheel. Stopped off for a Mac Attack on the way. The directions from Manchester to Swansea are: M56 onto M6 south onto M5 south-west onto M50 onto A40 to M4 west onto A48 onto A483. Not a problem.

Saturday 31 July: Swansea

First day of three-day match against Glamorgan as a lead-up to the fifth Test. We win toss and bat. Slats and Babs get us off to a good start. My knee is a bit sore, so ice up and have some treatment during the first session. Our innings turns into a run feast on the small ground and we're 4/400-plus when we declare an hour before stumps. Junior gets 152 not out including four 6s in one over.

We bowl 13 overs and get two wickets with Heals taking two catches – off me. Cracka bowls with plenty of pace on a slow, low wicket. Jump on bus back to hotel. Watch some TV and then go to bed feeling very tired both physically and mentally.

Please rain tomorrow.

Sunday 1 August: Swansea

Glamorgan bat until just after tea and declare at 8/363. At the end of play, we are 1/100 with Pistol 34 not out, and me 25 not out. After game have dinner with Sue, Warnie and Simone at the Castle Hotel in Neath. Catch a taxi back to Swansea about 9.15 pm and sit in the bar with the journos, who are buying the drinks tonight. Have a few beers and a couple of Bailey's and the discussion gets around to tomorrow's batting.

The bets start coming, so get out the diary and write them down.

Patrick Keane	*£10 for every six*
Malcolm Conn	*£20 for every six*
Brett (Ch. 9)	*£1 for every run*
Jim Tucker	*£100 if I run out AB*
Robert Craddock	*£50 if I hit a car*
Ken Casellas	*£5 for a cut for four*
Greg Baum	*£45 if I face up left-handed*

AB joins in and offers £100 if I can make a century. Out of all this, all I have to come up with is £10 if I don't add to my overnight score and £100 if AB runs me out.

Monday 2 August: Swansea

Easy money! I make 71 with three 6s. Let the cash flow! £136. Yeah! We declare at lunch with the score on 8/235. We take a few quick wickets and Cracka knocks over Maynard which kills the game. Glamorgan are 6/169 when rain washes out the last hour and a half. Jump on bus and head for Birmingham.

Watch a few videos on the bus, sleep, play cards, sleep. Have some room service on arrival then watch TV and sleep.

Australia 4/414 dec. (M. Waugh 152 not out, D. Boon 120, M. Slater 72) and 7/235 dec. (M. Hughes 71 not out, P. Reiffel 52) v. Glamorgan 8/363 dec. (S. Warne 4/67) and 6/169. Match drawn.

Tuesday 3 August: Birmingham

Train in morning. Very light workout, but everyone gets what they want out of the session. I bowl a bit off my short run then do some catching. Have some lunch back at the hotel after training. Sleep. Wake up and go to visit Sue.

Walk around town and drop into a curry place for dinner. Not bad. See Sue home to where she is staying. Back to the hotel about 10.30, watch Billy the Kid on TV, then sleep.

Wednesday 4 August: Swansea

Training in morning again, then sleep in afternoon. Down to team meeting at 6 pm. Bit of discussion about whether England will be different under new captain Atherton.

[At the same time, Atherton was talking about the Aussies and heaping praise on them, particularly Merv. In an interview on Test eve, he said, 'Test cricket is about toughness and temperament. It is about the Borders and the Boons – people who sell themselves dearly. And it's also about tough characters like Merv Hughes. I have enjoyed facing Merv very much because I have a lot of respect for him as a bowler. People talk about him in derogatory terms but he is a 200-wicket bowler and you cannot pull that down. In his own way, he is quite clever. At Lord's, where the wicket was very flat, he knew he needed something to unsettle us so he tried the chatter and the bouncers. At Trent Bridge, where the wicket was green, he put every ball in the right area. He didn't waste his time or effort. He didn't bother about the chatter because he didn't need it. People under-estimate him because of his appearance. They always under-value his contribution. In the first Test, he told me I hadn't improved in four years. I told him to get some new lines.'– IC]

Mr Border
   We are writing to say how disgusted we are with you. Why the hell don't you declare when you reach 300 and give England a chance to bat.
   You are a disgrace to your team, you are not fit to be a captain. You only think about yourself and nobody, I repeat, nobody else.
   You are a bastard, a pig, and everything else under the sun.
   And the rest of your team are just as bad. All England will be glad, yes, glad when you retire.
   Can't give you my full address - we are moving home today.
YOU BLOODY BASTARD. GET OUT OF ENGLAND.

Anon.
Sheffield

8 In the Home Straight

BACK in 1985, Merv's ambition was to score a Test run and play two Tests in a row. In his first Test against India at Adelaide he took 1/123 and was dropped. So much for the two Tests in a row. He was brought back a year later against England and dropped again. The two Tests in a row was still on hold and you could have named your own odds on Merv claiming 200 Test wickets *and* playing in 50 Tests. The rest, as they say, is history. Well, almost. Merv had chalked up the 200 wickets in the fourth Test at Headingley and all that remained was to reach the 50-Test milestone. The occasion arrived with the fifth Test at Edgbaston.

Thursday 5 August: Edgbaston

Down to the ground early for warm-up. Boys are keen to go on with the business and make it 4–0. No change to team from Headingley although Maysie has been under a bit of a cloud with a hamstring injury. He's been putting in a lot of work with Hooter to get the all-clear. Hooter comes out with a good line when he's asked about Maysie's fitness. 'I think he should be all right bowling, but I don't think he's going to be able to display that turn of pace he's got in the outfield.' AB and Simmo point out that we're going to have to cover for him in the field.

Atherton, in his first Test as captain, wins the toss and they bat. Gooch is back opening with Atherton, but not for long as Pistol gets him early, caught by Tubby at first slip. It's the first of five for Pistol with the one that bowls Hussain being a real gem. Junior chips in to bowl Smith while Warnie and Maysie get three between them. None for me, but I bowl OK.

Ice up knee after play then go back to hotel for room service and an early night.

Thursday 5 August: Melbourne

People were starting to say that the Test series no longer held any interest for them. 'I don't know if I can be bothered watching tonight,' a friend said. I begged to differ. There were many delights to savour, both from an individual and team point of view. A few examples: Shane Warne's tantalising leg spin, Mark Waugh's fluent batting, Australia's quest for another victory, Mike Atherton's debut as skipper, John Emburey's comeback and England's search for that tunnel with the light at the end of it.

I was ready for another night at home on the couch in front of the television. That is, until lunch when the ten-minute news break provided the opportunity to clean the teeth, whip on the pyjamas, turn on the bedroom TV and hop in to bed. On a couple of occasions, I stayed on the couch until tea, but in the depths of Melbourne's winter that meant using up too much firewood or power depending on which method of heating was favoured.

Apart from the warmth and comfort, going to bed after lunch also meant the TV telecast and the radio broadcast were in synchronisation. This allowed the true cricket fan to turn the TV sound down and listen to the radio coverage. I did this not only to quell Tony Greig's excited commentary but also to remind myself of those nights back in 1972 when the radio coverage was all we had. Those nights when Bob Massie took his 16 wickets at Lord's and Greg Chappell made one of the best hundreds ever seen. Which reminds me, when I was in England for the second and third Tests, it felt strange to hear the BBC radio coverage during the day because I was so used to hearing those voices at night.

Anyway, my belief that there was still plenty of interest in the Test series was proved correct especially when Paul Reiffel disposed of Graham Gooch early on the first day. And to see Mark Waugh get one through Robin Smith's defence was a joy. This brought Matthew Maynard to the crease. The boy from Glamorgan had come into the team with huge wraps after scoring a century off 73 balls against Australia at Neath five days earlier.

He was in a spot of bother immediately as Tim May's first delivery kicked and spun nastily, striking him in the groin. He lasted only ten balls before another delivery from May turned sharply into his pads and caught a glove on the way to Steve Waugh at silly mid-off. It was a perfect opening for the commentators to trot out the old favourite that cricket is a funny game. And, for good measure, we heard that 'five days is a long time in cricket' and 'you're only as good as your last innings'.

Friday 6 August: Edgbaston

Pistol makes it six wickets for himself when he gets Illot, the last man out. Emburey is 55 not out, a good knock. We lose Slats early, then Boonie goes for a duck. When Tubby and AB also go cheaply, we're 4/80 and in a bit of trouble. Tugga and Junior get their heads down for a 100-plus partnership. Junior makes a century and Tugga gives great support, the second time in the series that he has played a top innings when the pressure has been on.

Still 40-odd behind at stumps and we'll be looking to build a handy lead tomorrow because we'll have to bat last on a turning wicket.

Friday 6 August: Melbourne

They couldn't, could they? They, I mean England, couldn't bowl us out for 150 and set themselves up for a long-awaited win, could they? I wonder how many viewers started fearing the worst as Australia's top-order wickets fell quickly on the second day. You really do start to worry when David Boon goes for a duck. Actually, it's more than a worry, it's a disaster.

My preferred viewing position on the couch is a laid-back, feet-up reclining state with my head propped up by a cushion or two, but there was no way I could relax while the ball spun and the wickets toppled. It was sitting-bolt-upright, edge-of-the-seat stuff. Enter Mark Waugh, arguably the most relaxed batsmen I've ever seen. When he came in, the score might as well have been 2/339, not 2/39. Or 4/480, not 4/80, when his twin brother Steve joined him.

Mark played a couple of glorious cut shots against the spin in the early part of his innings and viewers immediately sensed that here was the man and here was the occasion. He departed four hours later having made 137 off 219 balls. The twelfth of his 18 boundaries took him past 100, his fourth century in Test matches. During the innings, he became the third Australian to pass 1000 runs on tour, behind David Boon and Michael Slater, but statistics tell only part of the story. It was the easy, confident manner in which he turned back the threat of the spinners that changed the course of the game.

The day wasn't devoid of drama for the Waughs. The England players believed fervently that Mark was caught at slip by Nasser Hussain off the bowling of Peter Such before he had scored, but umpire David Shepherd was unmoved. Later, Merv told me that there was a bit of verbal carry-on out in the middle as the England players had a few words to say to the batsman. 'I told them I didn't hit it,' Mark said after stumps were drawn. 'When they didn't let up, I wished I'd told them that I did hit it – that would have really annoyed them.'

Steve's contribution to the drama was to miss the second ball he received from Such. In turn, wicket-keeper Alec Stewart missed it and, in doing so, a stumping chance went begging. Around the lounge rooms of Australia, thousands of hearts jumped into thousands of mouths, then slowly settled back into their customary places. Later, when I turned off the TV, I headed for dreamland by counting Mark Waugh's boundaries like some people count sheep. For Alec Stewart, I imagined, there was no dreaming – just a nightmare.

Saturday 7 August: Edgbaston

Leave for ground at 9 am and have a hit in the nets to get my eye in. Don't have to wait long for a bat when play starts as Tugga goes for the addition of only two. Put on 100-odd with Heals who gets 80. Pistol and Warnie chip in and we get past 400 for a lead of 130-odd.

They bat again and Warnie gets Atherton. There's still a lot of cricket left in the game and much is going to depend on Warnie and Maysie.

Have a couple of beers in the bar back at the hotel, then up to room and order room service. Watch TV and sleep by about 11 pm.

Saturday 7 August: Melbourne

For the third night in a row, I leaned back in my favourite TV viewing spot, the couch. And over there in England, Merv leaned back and played his favourite batting stroke, the almighty smash over midwicket for six. It was his eighteenth such blow on the tour and a tremendous start to a marvellous partnership with Ian Healy. When Merv joined Healy at the fall of Steve Waugh's wicket, Australia was still 13 runs in arrears of England's first innings total; at lunch two hours later, the lead was almost 100.

Once again Merv had made a significant contribution to the Australian cause. He'd missed out with the ball, but he'd done something with the bat. That's the thing about Merv, you just can't keep him out of the game. He finished with 38 enormously valuable runs. In fact, this was an illustration of why the emphasis was on the word 'team' when the Australian team was talked about. Everyone made an important contribution at some stage of the series; there was no reliance on one or two players.

While Merv played the sheet anchor, Healy took up the attack to the England bowlers and scooted to 80 off 107 balls. During the pre-lunch session, my viewing was interrupted by a couple of phone calls, a boiling kettle and a crying baby. As a result, I was up and down from the couch like a jack-in-a-box and missed a few minutes here, a few minutes there. Often with Test cricket viewing, when you come back after these little breaks, you discover that nothing has changed. Not so with Healy at the wicket. For example, he went from the 40s into the 50s in the time it took me to go to the kitchen and turn off the kettle; from the 50s to the 60s while I went back to pour the tea.

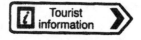

Sunday 8 August: Edgbaston

Get off to a great start when Warnie takes three wickets in five overs. The one that gets Gooch around his legs is another gem. Thorpe and Emburey hang around for a while before Maysie makes the breakthrough. Warnie and Maysie bowl long spells – about 50 overs each – while Pistol and myself send down 29 between us. No wickets for me again, but no-one hits me. We need 120 to win and Tubby and Slats wipe off eight before stumps.

Sunday 8 August: Melbourne

Sometimes, when watching Test cricket from England in the early hours of the morning, your eyes start to play tricks on you. I'll swear I once saw six stumps at each end of the wicket, but there might have been other contributing factors apart from a bout of tiredness. Anyway, I thought my eyes were playing tricks on me again when Shane Warne bowled Graham Gooch before lunch on the fourth day of this Test and I'll bet Gooch thought he was seeing things, too.

Warne was bowling around the wicket to Gooch and pitching the ball well outside leg stump. Gooch appeared to have perfected a tactic for handling this stuff by sliding his left leg down and across the wicket and deflecting the ball away with his pad. Nothing's going to happen here, I thought. But, then, I'm a long way from the action and unbeknown to me – and everyone else watching at home – Warne had cooked up a little plan.

He knew exactly what he was doing, unlike Robin Smith and Matthew Maynard who had already fallen during the morning to a combination of the Warne–May guile and English ineptitude against spin bowling. In fact, the score had not advanced from 3/115 following Maynard's dismissal when Warne's carefully-planned plot was hatched. He pitched one a long way outside leg to Gooch, so wide that Gooch couldn't get a pad to it. For a moment, the batsman must have thought he was in no harm, such was the width of the delivery. That was, until the ball took a savage change in direction as it bit and spun behind him and crashed into the stumps. Not content with producing one delivery described as 'the ball of the century', Warne had tossed in another contender for the title.

The Test match was as good as over there and then.

England's best batsman was out, four wickets were down and the deficit was still 17. Not to mention Warne's psychological hold over the opposition. To all those people who thought there was no interest in watching the cricket, let me tell you the Warne–May show that played into the early hours of the next morning was one of the highlights of the series. The rearguard action from Thorpe and Emburey stopped the wickets falling for a while, but it was worth staying awake waiting to see the next tantalising wicket-taking delivery.

Monday 9 August: Edgbaston

Win by eight wickets after losing Tubby and Slats early. Boys aren't too worried as Junior and Babsie put on another 100-run partnership to steer us home. Not a problem. Junior is Man of the Match.

Five Tests for four wins and a draw is a pleasing scoreline and we have a double celebration for the series result and winning this Test. The early finish gives us extra time to unwind before packing up and heading back to London.

Monday 9 August: Melbourne

Remember 1981? Remember Australia needing 130 to win a Test and being bowled out for 111 with big Bob Willis grabbing eight wickets. I remember sitting through that one in total disbelief. It couldn't happen again, could it? No, surely not. England didn't have a Bob Willis this time.

Mind you, when both openers fell to the spin of Such and Emburey with the score on 12, I seemed to be taken over by a strange sense of déjà vu. The heart started beating a trifle quicker and the palms were getting sweaty. Enter Mark Waugh for the second instalment of his free and easy batting display. The field was up and the outfield was empty, so Waugh lofted Such over the midwicket fence signalling that he was taking up where he left off in the first innings.

With David Boon proving that his first innings duck was an aberration and back to his best sheet-anchor role, knocking off the 120 for victory quickly became a stroll in the park. In fact, the way Waugh was batting, another century was his for the taking if the target had been 200.

Waugh deservedly won the Man of the Match award, but Shane Warne's impact on the game – especially with that dismissal of Gooch – could not be overlooked. Paying tribute to Warne after the match, skipper Allan Border said the England batsmen had become hopelessly enmeshed in the spinner's web. Their lack of adventure against Warne had enabled him to dictate terms to almost every batsman. 'If we had to bat against Shane we would do so a bit differently,' Border said. 'You don't see many English blokes running down the wicket to him. Our guys would try to get after him.'

Border revealed that one of the secrets to Warne's success was that he really gave the ball a rip. 'He has big strong hands,' he said. 'Other leg spinners in recent years have bowled the ball out of the back of their hands, but he tends to use more of his wrist and makes it come out the side, which increases his spin. I have always liked the way Shane bowls. When he came back for his second season in Test cricket, he had lost a bit of weight and it showed me he really wanted to be a Test cricketer.'

Heading off to bed when the telecast finished, I couldn't resist the temptation to try a few leggies as described by Border. I rummaged through my daughter's basket of toys and found a soft rubber ball. Coming in from the kitchen end of the hallway, I flicked the ball out of the back of the hand and gave it a bit of air. A bit too much actually. The ball clipped a light fitting and deflected on to a painting which crashed to the floor, thankfully with the glass intact.

My wife appeared at the bedroom doorway and offered a piece of excellent advice: 'Leave it to the experts.'

Australia 408 (M. Waugh 137, I. Healy 80, S. Waugh 59; P. Such 3/90, M. Bicknell 3/99) and 2/120 (M. Waugh 62 not out) d. England 276 (M. Atherton 72, J. Emburey 55 not out; P. Reiffel 6/71) and 251 (G. Thorpe 60; S. Warne 5/82, T. May 5/89) by 8 wickets. Man of the Match: M. Waugh.

The Australians were on top of the world after their eight-wicket win in the fifth Test put the series scoreline at 4–0 and the 1993 team was being hailed as the equal of the all-conquering 1989 outfit. However, performing these brilliant deeds had taken its toll both physically and mentally on the players.

Although he would never admit it publicly, the strain was telling on Merv. Apart from leading the charge with the ball, he was under pressure to keep up the daily entries in his diary. And it was the pages of the diary to which Merv turned to confess his private thoughts about the demands of the tour. Well, the demands of writing up the diary.

The entry for Tuesday 10 August, the day after the fifth Test, said it all:

August 1993

Week 32 • 222/143   Tuesday **10**

7.00

8.00

9.00   COVE — I'VE

10.00   HAD A GUT

11.00   FULL . . . .

12.00   4 — NILL

1.00

2.00

3.00   I'M NOT

4.00

5.00   DOING ANY

6.00   MORE!

7.00

November	December	January 1994	February	March	April

Our arrangement had been that Merv would photocopy the pages of the diary every couple of weeks, usually after the completion of a Test match, and post them to me. When I saw this one, I didn't know whether to laugh or cry. Eventually, I had a hearty chuckle to myself and figured that there wasn't much more to write about anyway. The high point of the series had been covered when the Ashes were retained with the win in the fourth Test at Headingley, a match that also produced individual highs such as Merv's 200th Test wicket and Border's undefeated double century.

Besides, Merv probably felt he didn't have a great deal to write about because of his match return of 0/77 off 37 overs at Edgbaston. And, as it turned out, he was to play in only one of the remaining two county fixtures before the team returned to London for their final engagement at the Oval.

That county match was against Essex, where Merv had played with the second XI ten years ago. He was keen to perform well at his former club, but the homecoming was spoiled by Derek Pringle who trapped Merv lbw for a duck. 'I never complain about umpiring decisions,' Merv said later. 'But I think I could have been given the benefit of the doubt just this once.'

Australia 4/391 dec. (S. Waugh 123, D. Martyn 105 not out, M. Taylor 78) and 0/34 dec. d. Kent 2/144 dec. and 222 by 89 runs.

Australia 6/357 dec. (M. Hayden 111, M. Waugh 108, A. Border 57) and 218 (B. Julian 66) v. Essex 268 (T. Zoehrer 3/57, T. May 3/71) and 9/277 (M. Waugh 3/26, T. Zoehrer 3/71). Match drawn.

WITH the absence of any diary entries from Merv, the task of completing the story of the tour is a bit difficult. On his return to Australia, I asked Merv to cast his mind back to events at the Oval from Thursday 19 August to Monday 23 August. 'You mean the Shane Warne Testimonial,' he said. 'Yeah, that was pretty big. Quite a few people turned up to see him get his Player of the Series award. It was a nice touch.'

There was something in the papers about Australia and England playing a Test match at the Oval during this period, but I didn't think that could be correct. That would have meant there had been six Tests and I was certain they only played five in a series. Mind you, I do seem to recall driving somewhere on the Thursday night and hearing Christopher Martin-Jenkins saying, 'If you're listening in Australia, I suggest you cover your ears because what I am about to say could be bordering on heresy – your Mr Hughes is getting a bit of stick.'

Merv getting a bit of stick? Now, that couldn't be right. I thought this must be a cricket nostalgia program that was replaying descriptions of Merv's first Test against England back in 1986. Why would I want to listen to that? I reached for the band selector and switched to FM.

Just to make sure, I checked my diary for 19–23 August and this is what I was doing at the time:

Thursday 19 August: Melbourne

Flew to Brisbane for a sports lunch. Long, tiring day. Home about 9 pm and returned a few phone calls. Sat down for late dinner. Played Tracy Chapman CD for background music. Bed about 11 and went to sleep as soon as head hit the pillow.

Friday 20 August: Melbourne

Slept in and had to rush to 3AW for guest spot on morning radio show. No time to read papers. Meetings all morning then out to lunchtime engagement. Home about 7 pm and missed the TV news. Dinner followed by a video.

Saturday 21 August: Geelong

Up early and down to Geelong for breakfast at a pub with a bunch of mates. It's an annual event on the day that Geelong clashes with Essendon. Talk football all morning. Go to game and see Geelong win by four goals. Celebrate at two pubs and a hamburger joint. Back to a mate's place to watch the World Athletics Championships being telecast from Stuttgart. Crash on couch.

Sunday 22 August: Melbourne

Sleep in then head home. Quiet day until friends drop in unexpectedly. One of those impromptu fun nights develops and we go out for dinner. Home about midnight for a port. Whack Willie Nelson's *Stardust* album on the stereo.

Monday 23 August: Country Victoria

Play with daughter and read her books instead of wasting time with the papers. Firewood stocks are running low so drive to the bush to pick up a load of wood. Visit brother, his wife and family. Stay for dinner and go to sleep on couch in front of the fire after big, home-cooked, country meal.

No cricket in that lot. Not a bat, a ball, a wicket or a run.

All right, all right. That's the end of the joke. It's gone on long enough and, yes, for the sake of our English readers, we have to admit there was a sixth Test at the Oval. And, yes, we must acknowledge that the home side broke through for their first win against Australia since the Boxing Day Test in Melbourne in 1986.

Merv's contribution was 3/121 and 3/110 to give him 31 wickets for the series, second only to Warne's 34. With the bat, he scored seven and 12, the latter innings being a defiant 86-minute stay as Australia battled to hold England at bay for as long as possible on the final day.

When he pulled Angus Fraser straight to Steve Watkin, Merv was left stranded one run short of yet another milestone, 1000 Test runs. His next run in Test cricket will make him only the third Australian player to take 200 wickets and score 1000 runs in Tests. The others are Richie Benaud and Ray Lindwall. Fine company that.

'When I got to 12, I had the choice of batting for another hour and a half and saving the game for my country or getting out and setting myself up to score the 1000th run in Australia,' Merv explained. Then he added, 'But I took the personal option.'

Australia 303 (I. Healy 83 not out, M. Taylor 70; A.Fraser 5/87, D. Malcolm 3/86) and 229 (S. Watkin 4/65, A. Fraser 3/44, D. Malcolm 3/84) lost to England 380 (G. Hick 80, A. Stewart 76, G. Gooch 56, M. Atherton 50; M. Hughes 3/121) and 313 (G. Gooch 79, M. Ramprakash 64; P Reiffel 3/55, S. Warne 3/78, M.Hughes 3/110) by 161 runs. Man of the Match: Angus Fraser.

P.S.

Returning home, Merv's chances of making that 1000th run on Australian soil were severely dented when he underwent knee surgery in early September. Expecting a straightforward clean-up on his troublesome right knee, Merv and his legion of fans were shocked to learn that the extent of the damage to his knee was worse than expected.

I visited him at the hospital on the afternoon of the operation to go over a few things for this book. Merv thought it would be an ideal time to talk because he would be sitting around doing nothing for a couple of hours before going home in the early evening. However, it was a somewhat glum Merv who greeted me in the day patients' lounge.

Before I could ask him about the operation, Merv put a question to me. 'Do sales of this book depend on me taking wickets?' he said. 'Well, you've taken 200, that's a pretty good start,' I replied, not quite tuning in to his line of inquiry. Then he explained, 'I won't be playing before Christmas.'

Instead of being sidelined for just six weeks, the normal lay-off after arthroscopic surgery, Merv was going to miss three Tests against New Zealand and probably the first Test against South Africa starting in Melbourne on Boxing Day. Given that the Sydney Test follows only a couple of days after the Melbourne Test, he seemed likely to miss that one, too.

If he couldn't make it back for any Tests in the Australian summer, Merv's aim was to get himself right for the three-Test tour of South Africa scheduled for early February 1994. If his courageous efforts of the Ashes tour were any guide, I'd love to put a bet on him being on the plane for South Africa.

At the hospital that afternoon I met Merv's father, Ian, for the first time since I'd seen him opening the bowling for Apollo Bay almost 30 years ago. Just as I'd seen where Merv gained his physical characteristics, I now discovered the origins of Merv's sense of humour. As we left the hospital, which is located at the top of steep hill, with Sue Hughes pushing her husband in a wheelchair, Ian Hughes said, 'Give it a shove and let him go.'

The Merv Hughes End-of-Tour Players Report

Allan Border

When a bloke's played over 100 Test matches, it gets pretty hard to say or write anything new about him. AB's still a tough competitor who leads by example and has the admiration and respect of all the players under him. AB had a great tour, topped off by making 200 not out in the fourth Test, winning the series and retaining the Ashes. And, for those people who think he hasn't got a sense of humour, AB was involved in some of the funnier moments. I've even got a photo to prove it. We had this thing going where players would try to stick the old two fingers up behind Simmo's head whenever someone was taking a photo of him. One day, I was focusing on Simmo as AB walked past. I didn't expect the skipper to put up the fingers, but, sure enough, up they went. It's a classic.

Mark Taylor

Tubby has been a reliable opener for Australia since breaking into the team against the West Indies in the 1988-89 season. He went through a slump last summer when the Windies toured, resulting in his being dropped to 12th man for the fifth Test in Perth. Fought back and showed everyone his tough, determined character.

Batted well, getting us off to good starts with Unit in the one-dayers and then with Slats during the Test series. This meant the top order was rarely exposed to the new ball. Tubby's century in the first Test when we were sent in to bat was as important an innings as was played during the Ashes campaign.

David Boon

The backbone of the Australian top order for the last few years, Babsie was making his third Ashes tour. On the previous two trips, he had failed to make a Test century and he was highly motivated to correct that situation. The breakthrough came when Babsie made 164 not out at Lord's and the floodgates were opened as centuries followed in the third and fourth Tests. Reinforced his reputation as one of the best short-leg fieldsmen around, taking some great catches. Off the field, his best performances were reserved for card games and renditions of the team song after the four Test wins.

Matthew Hayden

Selected for the tour after two great Sheffield Shield seasons with Queensland. I'd seen him play about a dozen times and he'd looked a pretty good player particularly the way he seemed to have plenty of time to play his shots against pace bowling. Also, he hits the ball very hard. Both these features were on show during the tour as Unit topped 1000 runs without playing a Test, the first Australian batsman to do so. His battle with Slats for the role as Tubby's opening partner brought out the best in both of them and was good for the team. While he missed the Tests, Unit had a taste of the big time when he opened in the one-day internationals. Funnily enough, his one-day efforts will be remembered for his sensational catch at deep point at Lord's rather than his batting.

Ian Healy

One of the best, no, the best wicket-keeper in the world. And a positive, aggressive batsman who regularly makes runs for us if we're in trouble. On the batting side, Heals made some quick runs in the one-dayers when they were needed and then made his first Test century in the first Test at Old Trafford. He scored the runs quickly in a fine partnership with Steve Waugh which gave us the time we needed to bowl out England a second time. Hardly made a mistake with the gloves, especially when keeping to the spinners which wasn't an easy task with Warnie turning the ball a long way and mixing up his deliveries. Finished with 26 dismissals, 21 caught and five stumped.

Wayne Holdsworth

Rated as the quickest bowler in Australia for the last couple of years, Cracka thrust his name in front of the selectors with a seven-wicket haul in the second innings of the 1992–93 Sheffield Shield final when New South Wales beat Queensland. Although he never really got his rhythm right in England, Cracka still worked very hard throughout the tour and showed what a terrific bowler he could be. I had the pleasure of rooming with him a couple of times and he was very entertaining company – a good bloke to have around the place. The TV was not required as Cracka was always on for a chat and the conversation was always about cricket. If he gets the chance to make his Test debut now that I'm injured, I hope he goes well. Not too well, of course.

Brendon Julian

Before the tour, I had played against BJ a couple of times although I really couldn't remember too much about him. The last time I saw him was a Shield match in Perth in January 1993 and he didn't do much. Not that he had to – we (the Vics) put in a shocker. In England, BJ was another of the young players to get a taste of the big time playing in the third one-dayer at Lord's and a couple of Tests. In his second spell in the one-dayer, he bowled so well that he took out the Man of the Match award. He then stepped up to Test ranks at Old Trafford and scored a duck. Cricket is like that. BJ missed the second Test, but was back for the third Test at Trent Bridge where he pulled off a magical caught and bowled to dismiss Robin Smith who was on fire. BJ also showed great maturity with his 57 not out in the second innings of that match when we were in a bit of trouble. A groin injury slowed him down at the end of the tour.

Craig McDermott

The outstanding bowler for Australia since getting back in to the side three years ago. His preparation for the Ashes tour was hampered by an operation after the New Zealand tour in March. He'd taken 13 wickets in the three Tests in New Zealand amid reports that he was carrying an injury, a fact confirmed by the operation. In England, Billy appeared to have thrown off the after-effects with his displays in the one-day series when he was named Man of the Match in the first one and Australia's Player of the Series. Going into the Tests with 198 Test wickets to his name, Billy's 200 looked a formality. However, he failed to take a wicket despite bowling well in the first Test and was rarely sighted after that.

Damien Martyn

A young player with experience already in Test matches, one-dayers and tours, Marto wasn't exactly a rookie although that's probably how a lot of people saw him. Along with Unit and Slats, Marto is a batsman with a big future in the game. He's an aggressive type who loves to take on the bowling, a trait on display when he played in the third one-day international at Lord's and made a very good 50 not out. The wealth of in-form batting talent in the squad meant he didn't play another big game after that, but he made heaps in the county games. Marto also showed off his all-round ability by bowling some handy medium pace stuff, fielding very well and even keeping wickets.

Tim May

Although he was a member of the Ashes tour in 1989, injuries had prevented Maysie from establishing a regular spot for himself in the Australian team in recent years. However, a brilliant performance against the West Indies in Adelaide during the 1992–93 summer gave him another chance to tour England. With 21 wickets in five Tests, Maysie looks like he's in the team to stay now, particularly as he bowled so well in tandem with Warnie. Off the field, for me, one of the highlights of the tour was rooming with Maysie. He has great taste in music and a fine sense of humour. Great company who was always keen to have an Indian feed and a few beers.

Paul Reiffel

If you ask me, Pistol has been under-rated by many Victorians for too long. His success in England should change all that. Had a slow start to the tour playing in the first two one-dayers before being omitted for the final match. Troubled for a while by no-balls and a lack of rhythm, but it all came together when he was picked for the fourth Test. In three Tests, Pistol took 19 wickets, better than any England player managed in the entire series. Even so, I reckon if you asked Pistol for his tour highlight it'd have nothing to do with his bowling. I wouldn't mind betting that it was the six he hit off Derek Pringle in the county match against Essex because it was the first six he's ever hit in first-class cricket. One of the real success stories along with Slats and Warnie.

Michael Slater

Before the tour I'd never seen Slats bat. I knew all about his outstanding season with New South Wales in which he scored 1000-plus runs and I had heard that he was a very aggressive player with a tight defence. On a trip to Wagga Wagga with one of my sponsors, I was quizzed by the locals as to what I thought of Michael's batting style. I replied, 'Does he bat right or left-handed?' When I finally got to see him batting in England, I was very impressed. He got among the runs early and, although overlooked for the one-dayers, he nudged out Matthew Hayden for the opening spot with Tubby in the first Test and didn't look back. He scored a half-century on debut and followed up with a magnificent 152 in the second Test at Lord's. His form dropped off towards the end of the tour, but he wasn't Robinson Crusoe on that.

Shane Warne

A big improver last summer, Warnie set himself up for England with a fine tour of New Zealand in March where he took 17 wickets in three Tests. The pressure was on him because it was felt that Warnie could be a real match winner. Fortunately, for him and the team, he went from strength to strength and couldn't put a foot wrong. Bowled very well from his first ball in a Test on English soil until the last ball of his 40th and final over in the sixth Test. All up, Warnie sent down 440 overs in six Tests and captured 34 wickets at 25.79. By the way, only 877 runs were scored off him which is extremely economical for a leg spinner. Away from the cricket grounds of England, Warnie took everything in his stride including the enormous attention he received from the media and the public. Warnie has slotted into the Australian team as if he's been there for years.

Mark Waugh

When batting well – and on this tour that was often – Junior is up there with the best in the world. His lengthy apprenticeship with New South Wales and Essex seems to have done wonders for him. Throw in the fact that Junior's catching and fielding is nothing short of sensational and that he is a handy bowler and you have one heck of a cricketer. The runs flowed for Junior and he was one of four batsmen to pass 1000 runs for the tour. He also topped the sixes list with 26. His 137 in a pressure situation during the fourth Test was outstanding, but he's another player who might not nominate the obvious as his tour highlight. No, I reckon he'd say it was opening the bowling in both innings at Lord's.

Steve Waugh

An important player for Australia over the last six or seven years in both Tests and one-day games. Like his twin brother, Steve's ability with the bat and ball and in the field makes him a fine cricketer. A joy to watch when he's in full flight with the bat, hitting the ball with great power. However, Tugga curbed his own game in the second innings of the first Test, allowing Heals to score his maiden Test ton before the declaration. As well as helping Heals to his century, Tugga's role in the partnership set up a win for us. Another example of Tugga's value to the team came in the third Test when he batted solidly with BJ to force a draw. Finally, when Tugga let himself go, he made 157 not out in the fourth Test, putting on an unfinished 332 stand with AB. Topped the averages with 416 runs at 83.20.

Tim Zoehrer

Ziggy has the happy knack of being in the right place at the right time. He seems to make runs and do well behind the stumps for Western Australia every time there is an Ashes tour coming up. In recent years, he has added another string to his bow by becoming a useful leg spinner. Those leggies helped him to top the bowling averages for the second Ashes tour in a row. His main role on tour was as a back-up for Heals, but he almost gained selection – as a bowler – for the fifth Test when Maysie was in doubt because of a hamstring injury. That could have been very interesting as Ziggy is a fierce competitor.

Bob Simpson (coach)

In charge for about eight years, so he must be doing something right. Forms a tough leadership combination with AB. It's always a treat to be involved in Simmo's fielding drills and high balls at training – as long as someone else is running after them. Seriously, Simmo works the team very hard in catching drills and I reckon that aspect of our preparation helps put us ahead of the rest.

Errol Alcott (physiotherapist)

For Hooter, a tour usually turns out to be a holiday, but not this time. Early on, he had to get Maysie and myself back to match fitness which was no mean feat. It didn't stop there with Heals (thumb), Maysie (knee, hamstring), me (groin), Babsie (knee), Billy (groin), Ziggy (whole body), BJ (groin), Warnie (elbow, shoulder) and Pistol (achilles) to look after at various stages. When he did get time off from the players, he had Simmo and manager Des Rundle lining up for treatment. Did a great job and should be commended on his efforts.

Des Rundle (team manager)

Affectionately known as 'Ger' (short for manager), Des did a good job. He was always put under as much pressure as possible by the players particularly when it came to the organisation of tickets for guests. Always came through with the goods even if it was at the last minute. Arguably his toughest job, though, was getting through 18 holes of golf on the day after a Test victory.

Mike Walsh (scorer)

Mike, on his second Ashes tour, was always there to lend a hand to the players. Being from Victoria, he's an Aussie Rules supporter and an Essendon one at that. As a Footscray fan, I locked horns with him on a couple of occasions. The highlight of his tour would have been sitting next to me on the flight from Melbourne to London. On the day that we left, Footscray beat Essendon and I told Mike all about it for the next 24 hours.

Merv's Tour Bests

Best innings by an Australian

Allan Border's 200 not out, fourth Test at Headingley.

Best innings by an England player

Robin Smith's 167 not out in the first one-dayer at Edgbaston.

Best wicket taken by an Australian

That ball. Shane Warne's first ball to Mike Gatting, first inning of the first Test at Old Trafford.

Best wicket taken by Merv Hughes

That *other* ball. The last ball of the fourth day of the first Test that bowled Gatting.

Best wicket taken by an England bowler

Phil Tufnell getting Mark Waugh on 99 in the second Test at Lord's.

Best catch by an Australian

Mark Waugh to dismiss Alec Stewart off Paul Reiffel, second innings of the fourth Test at Headingley.

Best catch by an England player

Nasser Hussain to dismiss Allan Border off Peter Such, first innings of the fifth Test at Edgbaston.

Best run-out (allcomers)

Mike Atherton on 99 in the England second innings during the second Test at Lord's. [He slipped mid-pitch and was beaten by a big throw from the outfield by Merv.]

Best Australian fieldsman

Mark Waugh.

Best England fieldsman

Nasser Hussain.

Best ground

Lord's.

Best pitch

Lord's.

Best crowd

Old Trafford, Manchester, first Test. [The crowd responsible for Merv's 'Sumo' tag.]

Best umpire

All of them.

Best six by Merv

The one off Derek Pringle in the first one-dayer at Old Trafford.

Best six by anyone else

The big-hitting Mark Taylor in full flight during the first Test at Old Trafford when he put Peter Such over the rope – just.

Best dressed Australian cricketer (on-field)

Mark Waugh. [Especially wearing those sunnies with the white arms.]

Best dressed Australian cricketer (off-field)

Matthew Hayden. Lived up to his nickname 'Unit' which is short for 'good-looking unit'.

Best first-release movie

Jurassic Park.

Best video (on bus or in hotel)

Wayne's World.

Best hotel (stayed at or visited)

Westbury, London.

Best beer

XXXX.

Best restaurant

A tie between a Mexican place in London called Break for the Border and Planet Hollywood.

Best nightclub

Long Island Tee Shop, London.

Best city or town visited

Oxford.

Best golf course

Moor Park, London.

Best golfer

Mark Taylor.

Best card player

David Boon (the best and most sensible).

Best dancer

Wayne Holdsworth in the dressing room doorway at Northampton.

Best singer

No-one in our squad qualifies.

Best eater

Without doubt – me!

Best drinker

All seventeen after a Test win.

Best joke teller

Tim May.

Tour Statistics

TEST MATCHES

Bowler	M	O	Mdns	Runs	Wkts	Av.	5wi	10m	Best
I.J. Cover	-	-	-	-	-	-	-	-	-
M.G. Hughes	6	296.2	78	877	31	27.26	1	-	5/92

Batsman	M	Inn	NO	Runs	Av.	HS	50s	100s	Ct
I.J. Cover	-	-	-	-	-	-	-	-	-
M.G. Hughes	6	5	-	76	15.20	38	-	-	-

FIRST-CLASS GAMES

Bowler	M	O	Mdns	Runs	Wkts	Av.	5wi	10m	Best
I.J. Cover	-	-	-	-	-	-	-	-	-
M.G. Hughes	14	470.2	113	1420	48	29.58	1	-	5/92

Batsman	M	Inn	NO	Runs	Av.	HS	50s	100s	Ct
I.J. Cover	-	-	-	-	-	-	-	-	-
M.G. Hughes	14	12	3	299	33.22	71	2	-	3

NON-FIRST-CLASS GAMES

Bowler	M	O	Mdns	Runs	Wkts	Av.	5wi	10m	Best
I.J. Cover	1	-	-	-	-	-	-	-	-
M.G. Hughes	-	-	-	-	-	-	-	-	-

Batsman	M	Inn	NO	Runs	Av.	HS	50s	100s	Ct
I.J. Cover	1	-	-	-	-	-	-	-	-
M.G. Hughes	-	-	-	-	-	-	-	-	-